Scott Allan is an international bestselling author of over 30 personal growth and self-development books published in 12 languages. He is the author of *Fail Big, Undefeated*, and *Do the Hard Things First*.

A former corporate business trainer in Japan and transformational mindset strategist, Scott has invested over 10,000 hours of research and instructional coaching in the areas of self-mastery and leadership training.

With an unrelenting passion for teaching, building critical life skills, and inspiring people around the world to take charge of their lives, Scott Allan is committed to a path of constant and never-ending self-improvement.

Many of the success strategies and self-empowerment materials that are reinventing lives around the world have evolved from Scott Allan's 20 years of practice and teaching critical skills to corporate executives, individuals and business owners.

You can contact Scott at:
www.scottallanbooks.com

Books by Scott Allan

Empower Your Thoughts

Drive Your Destiny

Relaunch Your Life

The Discipline of Masters

Do the Hard Things First

Undefeated

No Punches Pulled

Fail Big

Rejection Reset

Built for Stealth

Check out the complete collection of books and training here:
www.scottallanbooks.com

How to Choose Yourself First and Take
Charge of Your Life by Confidently
Asking For What You Want

SCOTT ALLAN

Published by
Rupa Publications India Pvt. Ltd 2025
7/16, Ansari Road, Daryaganj
New Delhi 110002

Sales Centres:
Bengaluru Chennai
Hyderabad Jaipur Kathmandu
Kolkata Mumbai Prayagraj

Copyright © Scott Allan 2025

The views and opinions expressed in this book are the author's own and the facts are as reported by him which have been verified to the extent possible, and the publishers are not in any way liable for the same.

All rights reserved.
No part of this publication may be reproduced, transmitted, or stored in a retrieval system, in any form or by any means, electronic, mechanical, photocopying, recording or otherwise, without the prior permission of the publisher.

P-ISBN: 978-93-7003-321-4
E-ISBN: 978-93-7003-018-3

First impression 2025

10 9 8 7 6 5 4 3 2 1

Printed in India

This book is sold subject to the condition that it shall not, by way of trade or otherwise, be lent, resold, hired out, or otherwise circulated, without the publisher's prior consent, in any form of binding or cover other than that in which it is published.

Contents

Introduction: Living the Rejection Free Journey   ix

Part 1
Choose Yourself First

1. Debunking the Lies of Rejection	3
2. Choosing a Life Over a Life of Rejection	12
3. Defeating Your Rejection Persona	21
4. Self-Rejection and Those Old Voices	29
5. Redefining Your Personal Value	34
6. Breaking Free of the Predictable Path	42
7. Rejection and Love Dependency	50

Part 2
Just Ask for It!

8. Why We Fear Asking	61
9. Essentials to Asking for What You Want	72
10. Simple Strategies for Asking	78
11. Asking for Help	87

Part 3
The Power of Desensitization

12. Desensitization and the Flooding Process	95
13. Getting Desensitized to Rejection	101
14. No More Excuses	107

Conclusion: Building the Rejection Free Lifestyle   114

"Perhaps we shall learn, as we pass through this age, that the 'other self' is more powerful than the physical self we see when we look in the mirror."

—**Napoleon Hill,** author of
Think and Grow Rich

Introduction:
Living the Rejection Free Journey

"Confront the dark parts of yourself, and work to banish them with illumination and forgiveness. Your willingness to wrestle with your demons will cause your angels to sing."

—**August Wilson**, American Playwright

First of all, I want to do two things: I want to welcome you to this book, Rejection Free, and I want to say thank you. You have just taken a positive step in taking charge of your life, and I am happy to have you here.

I wrote this book because I know the power that rejection has in all of our lives. Left unchecked, rejection can control our choices and influence our decisions. Left unchecked, rejection eventually kills our dreams.

You may live in fear of rejection, as I did for many decades. But it doesn't have to be this way. In this book, I show you that you can conquer your fears, become anything you want, and do anything you want without living in fear. Whatever rejection issues you have can and will be overcome. I want you to know that you are not alone in this journey.

Fear of rejection can be a very isolating emotion. In order to protect ourselves, we covert our emotions and stay hidden, like little children under the covers afraid of the dark. We try to "play it safe" and take fewer risks.

The problem with this is that we give up life-changing opportunities, ideas, and chances to avoid the pain that rejection brings. This pain not only causes emotional trauma, but for many of us it can be as frightening as facing physical injury or even death.

As rejects, we become like chameleons in a large jungle: fearful of being discovered by predators, we become adept at blending in, transforming, and disappearing. Ashamed to show who we really are, we reject ourselves by staying out of sight. If they can't find you, they can't judge or condemn you.

The jungle is the perfect place to stay out of sight. That means less social pressure. We can stay under the radar without being asked to do anything outside of our comfort zone. By staying out of sight, you avoid being judged or criticized. We have adapted to a lifestyle that has become our survival zone.

Many of us have convinced ourselves that life is better this way. By hiding from painful situations where there is a possibility of being judged, ridiculed or condemned, we can control our environment through avoidance. This is not a way to live, it is a way to survive.

Let me ask you this: What opportunities or dreams have you given up to stay hidden? What do you regret not doing because the fear of being ostracized or rejected was just too much to face?

Rejection is a very real experience. For people who have attached a deeper, more personal emotion to rejection, it can be completely terrifying.

Consider these questions:

- What would you do right now if you removed your fear of rejection? What acceptable risks would you be willing to take? What opportunities would you explore?

- What would you succeed at and commit to if you could remove your feelings of shame? What ideas would you pursue? What would you create?
- How do you see your life changing as you push through your personal pain of rejection?
- Can you envision a life where you are free of your rejection issues once and for all?
- Do you struggle to please people only to end up more alone and confused?
- How often do you challenge your fear of being embarrassed?
- Do you turn down speaking opportunities?
- Do you stay in relationships because you are afraid to risk something or someone new?
- Do you hold back from asking for the things you really want for fear of being told no?

Rejection is not exclusive to one person or group of people. It is something we all experience. The difference is how we handle it.

For years I avoided any situation that threatened my ego-sensitive self. If I was denied something I wanted, it was a personal attack on my character. If someone criticized me or made a disparaging remark, it was because I deserved it for being a "less than. By making it personal, I became more fearful. As we will see later in this book, rejection comes in many forms and disguises.

In Rejection Free, we will learn the specific strategies for how to:

- Choose yourself first, no matter what people think of you
- Ask for what you want without fear of hearing NO
- Break free from rejection in any situation that requires you to be brave and face your fears

- Stop trying to please the wrong people and start paying attention to the right ones.
- Realize that rejection isn't all about you (and how inspiring that is!)
- End the trap of predictability and how it hurts your chances for success
- Overcome your self-doubt and become great at asking for what you want most.
- Boost your confidence and take charge of your life.
- Desensitize yourself to rejection so you can handle anything that comes your way!

Rejection happens to everyone. No one is immune to it. But every time rejection tries to defeat you, you can use the techniques and strategies in this book to defeat rejection instead.

You can learn to free yourself from feelings of shame and fear of loss. By taking action in the face of fear, you free yourself from an emotional roller coaster and learn to live your life with confidence.

Now, just to be clear, this book isn't about how to avoid rejection. Rejection Free is designed to put you in charge of your life by dealing with life's situations when you are faced with rejection.

When we have developed the life skills to deal with fearful situations, we can move from retreat to action. This book will teach you how to turn your experience of rejection into an advantage.

Here are some everyday examples of rejection at work:

- You ask for a raise or a vacation at work and your manager says NO, your performance has been below average.
- You finally get up the nerve to ask that girl you've been watching for six months out on a date...and then she walks by you on the street with another guy.

- The new book you just published has four reviews, and three of them are negative.
- The bank says NO to your loan application because you don't make enough money.
- The dream job you're counting on goes to someone younger.
- You ask someone for help and they say NO.
- Your spouse of twenty years suddenly files for divorce.
- Your presentation that you've been working on for months has people walking out.

Building the Rejection-Free Lifestyle

I'm inviting you on a journey: It's a journey to a greater sense of freedom. It's a guided plan to give you the techniques and deeper awareness to deal with rejection instead of trying to escape and avoid it. We can't escape it, but we can free ourselves from falling into self-pity and the pain of regret for missed opportunities later in life.

Over the years, I have discovered that taking fewer risks to avoid rejection is not an escape plan, but can become a way to quietly fail. Less risk means less of everything. The risks I am talking about are the opportunities we miss and ignore for fear of losing what we have.

But it doesn't have to be this way

There is a solution. It is not as difficult as you may think. The way out for you is so close, you are almost there. But you will have to take action and get your hands dirty.

Your other option is to continue to live in fear. If you are reading this book, I assume you want the tools to deal with rejection and be free of the power it has over you.

Breaking out of your fear-based comfort zone - your protective cocoon - isn't always easy, but it is possible. If it were easy, we would all do it. But good things come to those who try and persevere.

People do it every day. Look around you. Find someone who has recently succeeded at something.

We have this idea that all the successful people out there are somehow better than us. They have tons of confidence and support, and from the outside it seems like their success is guaranteed.

But that's just not true

People who get where they want to go do so by pushing through their fear. History is full of successful entrepreneurs, authors, actors, and musicians who struggled with rejection for years and many times before they got where they wanted to be.

Harland David Sanders, better known as Colonel Sanders of Kentucky Fried Chicken, had a hard time selling his chicken at first. His famous secret chicken recipe was rejected 1,009 times before a restaurant finally accepted it.

Charlie Chaplin was initially rejected by Hollywood studio heads who thought his style of comedy and acting was too silly to ever be popular or entertaining.

A newspaper editor fired Walt Disney because "he lacked imagination and had no good ideas. After that, Disney started a series of businesses that ended in bankruptcy and failure. By persevering and moving forward, Disney's "lack of imagination" created a multi-billion dollar empire that is enjoyed by millions of children and adults every year.

Albert Einstein, who didn't speak until he was four and

couldn't read until he was seven, was expelled from school and denied admission to the Polytechnic School in Zurich. Teachers and parents believed he was slow and mentally retarded. Einstein went on to win the Nobel Prize and his work and theories changed the face of modern physics.

One of the most successful television talents in history and one of the richest women in the world, Oprah Winfrey, was fired as a television reporter for being "unfit" for television.

In this book, we will learn to:

- Take action when you are afraid.
- Take action to break the specific fear of rejection.
- Take action when you are paralyzed and feel helpless.
- Desensitize your fear of rejection by doing the thing that scares you.

You may think, "But what action should I take? You say 'take action' as if it were an easy thing to do. I would take action, but I don't know where to start."

Let's take it one step at a time. We start with small steps. You don't have to jump in the ocean and expect to swim to the other side of the Atlantic, but you do have to get your feet wet.

Take small actions every day to defeat something that scares you, and rejection loses its power. In the end, this is what we want: to reduce the power of your fear-based self; to empower you to build a new mindset that strips away all self-doubt.

This can be done. You can do it

If you are willing to risk yourself by putting the "real you" out there, you could end up creating a specific situation that significantly changes your life. When you take action and do what you are most afraid of, you are taking charge of your life and your destiny.

By not risking, you risk more. When you hide, you stay afraid

If you isolate yourself from your pain, as we often do, it increases the pain of being alone and increases the experience of rejection. There is risk in everything.

There is risk in doing nothing and there is risk in doing something. Everything has consequences and rewards. We win and we sometimes fail. Let's focus on winning together and breaking free of the emotional chains that keep you trapped.

The ball is in your court.

It's time to play.

PART 1

CHOOSE YOURSELF FIRST

1
Debunking the Lies of Rejection

"I know that when a door closes, it can feel like all doors are closing. A rejection letter can feel like everyone will reject us. But a closed door leads to clarity. It's really an arrow. Because we cannot go through that door, we will go somewhere else. That somewhere else is your true life."

—Tama J. Kieves

Rejection is full of lies that we believe about ourselves. One of the first steps to recovery and creating a rejection-free lifestyle is to break free of these lies by being completely honest with ourselves. By aligning our thoughts and ideals with reality, we create less resistance for ourselves.

These lies keep us from achieving the happiness and freedom we could have. The lies are what keep you trapped and continue the pattern of living in the hell of rejection. This is a term I coined for when we are so afraid of rejection because of our insecurities that we walk around expecting it from everyone.

As long as you act, behave and think differently than the person you want to be, you are living these lies every day.

Lies, myths and half-truths

For the most part, I have always believed that there was something wrong with me, that my rejection was a disease that only I had contracted; the rest of the world was perfect and I was flawed. But if you question that logic, you can begin to see the lies behind the broken belief.

We all buy into the lies that perpetuate and support this condition. If you convince yourself that you're not good enough, you'll always be trying to prove yourself to someone. Even after you've had some big wins, you'll chalk it up to "I just got lucky."

We are flawed in the sense that we have a hard time accepting ourselves as we are; there is this obsession to be more, to have more, or to prove that we have value and worth. But it's like trying to fill a bucket with a hole in the bottom.

Big Lie #1: I have to agree with everyone and value their opinions above all else

If you agree with everyone, you don't agree with anyone. You're trying to make friends and please everyone on both sides of the fence; if people find out that you just say what they want to hear, no one will value your opinion or pay attention to you. What will happen is that you'll end up being rejected again, only this time by your own doing.

We want to be liked, valued, and recognized as having a place in this world. But the basic truth is that not everyone will like you. They may just want something from you, like a favor, so the approval you get from temporary kindness doesn't always last.

When you start thinking long-term and supporting the people who are your true friends, you can stop pretending to be popular and focus on being yourself. By focusing on delivering value to people, we attract the kind of friends and relationships that matter.

Big Lie #2: Being rejected is personal and means there is something wrong with me

The power of rejection is only as strong as you choose to make it. Two people can be rejected for the same thing: one takes it personally and gives up; the other says, "Okay, who's next?" and keeps going. You have to keep going if you want to break free.

It doesn't matter if you ask someone out and they say no. It doesn't matter if you apply for twenty jobs and they all say no. It doesn't matter if you write a book and thirty publishers kick it out the door. The rejection you experience, which basically says, "You're no good," either makes you or breaks you.

In the end, how you perceive the experience has everything to do with how you're going to react to it. "Rejection" is your opinion (your own judgment of your experience), not someone else's.

If someone doesn't like your character or the way you look or act, just remember that those same people aren't perfect either. Have you ever rejected anyone?

Think back to a time when you did, and then find out why. It is this belief at the heart of it all - the belief that "I am inferior to the rest of the world" - that keeps us trapped in a state of rejection.

We will go into this more later in the book, but one of the biggest lies about rejection that everyone buys into is that it is personal. It's the "I wasn't chosen because there's something wrong with me" syndrome. More often than not, what looks and feels personal has to do with the other person and nothing to do with you.

There are times, painfully so, when we are rejected for personal reasons. We're too tall, we're not educated enough, or we just don't have the right personality for the job.

But in many situations, we are rejected for reasons beyond our control that have more to do with the other person. The person who rejects you has his or her own personal reasons that go beyond us. In fact, as I have experienced, what I initially perceived as a personal attack on my character was actually someone else's decision based loosely on emotion.

So, take comfort in knowing that no matter how painful your rejection may have been, we can't always control or be responsible for other people's choices.

Big Lie #3: Rejection is a permanent condition I was born with

Everyone is at a different stage of the process regarding their rejection issues. For many, it lasts through high school and then they grow out of it; on the other hand, some people live with it their whole lives. But until you have faced and dealt with your fear of rejection, you will always be afraid of being rejected or told no. For many, fear of rejection exists as a permanent condition if untreated.

If you grew up in a home that was critical, harsh, and controlling, your rejection issues may run deep and stay with you throughout your life, resulting in perfectionistic behavior and thinking that perpetuates the cycle. Constant criticism damages your self-esteem and undermines your self-confidence at an early age.

If you have been through this, your rejection issues are unlikely to go away until you take action and do the things you are now afraid to do. Rejection isn't permanent for anyone; sometimes you get a YES and many times you don't. No one is exempt. What makes the difference is your response to a rejection moment.

Do you believe you were born to be rejected? Or do you see it as something you have contracted, like a virus for which there is no cure? The message I want to share with you now and throughout this book is this: People are as rejected as they choose to be.

You can control the outcome of any situation where rejection is an issue. You have the choice to let it defeat you or to empower you.

Big Lie #4: I'm different and weird, so I'll be rejected

Everyone is weird in their own unique way. When we try too hard to be normal, it puts stress and pressure on us to perform. You have been taught that there is such a thing as "normal" in this world, but that's a lie. There isn't a norm. This leads to perfectionism. You are not rejected because you are different.

You're being rejected by yourself because you're trying too hard to be something you're not; you're trying too hard to be "normal," a word used by people who are too afraid to be themselves. The next time you look at something and label it as weird, it could just be that you are measuring it to fit your own "normal" version of reality.

Your denial persona is obsessed with "normal." It has its own built-in "normal" radar, so when you start acting or doing something out of the ordinary, it raises red flags and pulls you back. You may feel embarrassed or humiliated when you do something strange. You may not be aware of it because you have spent most of your life trying to act normal.

When you are severely criticized for being you, you become conditioned over the years not to act weird - it is not acceptable. "Normal people do this." "Normal is like this." That's a lie. There is conformity, and as long as you're conforming to someone else's vision of how you should act and behave, you're throwing away your uniqueness and settling for boring instead of unique.

Big Lie #5: If Only I Were Better, Smarter, and More Likeable, or, The Self-Denial Persona

You need to distinguish between the projections others make on you and what is actually true. I know the world we live in looks different. We see supermodels, rock stars, and actors buying lavish homes and receiving hordes of attention. We feel cheated. Where is my share? Why was I born different?

A friend of mine once said to me, "You can't be like Jeff Bezos. There is only one Jeff Bezos, and that job is taken." He was right. The best we can hope for is to be true to ourselves.

For years, I compared myself to other people. Not happy with who I was, I wanted to be someone else. I thought I was the problem. But when you think like that, you reject yourself before anyone else can.

- If only I had what he had...
- If only I could be in his position...
- If only I were good enough...
- Why is this happening to me again?
- Why am I always left out?
- There, you see? I have been rejected again ...

These expectations we have created are not of our own making. We are trying to fulfill the expectations that were placed on us in our childhood. Do you remember? The pressure to perform, to be better, to try harder so you wouldn't disappoint someone, most likely an older sibling or your parents.

As long as you're trying to live up to what you think others expect of you, you're still living the same pattern over and over again. You are trying to recreate what you failed to do in the past. Only now, instead of trying to make someone else happy - which you know is impossible - you have put the pressure on yourself.

Self-expectations are the most damaging because we don't realize that we are the ones who set the bar for ourselves. We've convinced ourselves that someone else is expecting this of us.

Big Lie #6: I can't be successful because I keep getting rejected, and rejection is a sign that I should give up and pursue something else

You have the right to be you. By choosing yourself instead of rejecting who you are, the Big Lies are cast aside. What lies are those? I am not worthy or capable of being or doing what I am passionate about. I don't deserve recognition. I am strange and socially awkward.

All lies. Sure, maybe there is some truth to them: Maybe you are socially awkward. Maybe you are lacking in some area of your life that needs to be developed. Maybe you have self-esteem issues. But who doesn't have these weaknesses? Growing up, we had people close to us who rejected us because of our imperfections, and that carried over into our adult lives. But now we still believe that rejection exists because we're not good enough or somehow inferior.

Remember what Henry Ford said: *"Whether you think you can or you think you can't, you're right."*

What you think and believe becomes who you are. You will act on your thoughts and make your beliefs real. If you give up every time you experience rejection, whether it is personal or business, you close the doors to success.

The key is to push through the fear and adapt to the

pain. This may sound like "motivational hype," but it is the surefire strategy that works. Later we will look at the strategy of desensitization and how you can make yourself stronger, better, and more adept at handling whatever comes your way.

It takes time to work through these lies we have about ourselves. But as we move through this book and you have time to reflect on what you are learning, you will begin to see a new set of truths emerge.

Our thoughts and beliefs have been corrupted over the years. By rejecting who we are, we have failed to become who we most wanted to be. This is the ultimate form of self-rejection.

Spend twenty minutes each day in silence. Schedule this time if necessary. During this time, explore your feelings and thoughts. Question your beliefs about yourself. Try to see the lies through the negative emotions you are holding on to.

Committing to a daily habit of self-exploration can open your awareness and encourage you to transform the lies that keep you trapped.

"Always bear in mind that your resolution to succeed is more important than any other thing."

—Abraham Lincoln

2

Choosing a Life Over a Life of Rejection

"We shouldn't romanticize rejection. There's nothing romantic about rejection. It's horrible."

—Marlon James

A mentor of mine once said to me, "If you want to make serious changes in your life, you need to create a vision of the person you would most like to be. It has to be someone you admire and look up to. Someone you want to be friends with and model yourself after. Someone who inspires you. Create this persona and then put all your efforts into becoming that person.

And so...

I created Bob.

What about Bob?

Bob hates his job. He hates his life.

He has worked in the same office for fifteen years and lives a menial existence. He comes to work, clocks in, clocks out, and then at the end of the day he goes home to a small one-bedroom apartment. He watches a lot of TV and tries not to think about things.

Bob has lost a lot of hope over the years. Sometimes he thinks he doesn't have much to live for. But Bob has never tried to find another job. He's never tried to change things because he's chosen to accept life as it is and retreat from reality.

Bob has never tried anything else that might make him happier. He never takes chances or tries to meet new people. Bob lives a menial existence, and the worst part is, he knows it.

Every day is the same, day in and day out, even though he hates it. It makes no sense. His wife left him because he was so unhappy. He lost a lot of friends when he became cynical and depressed.

You see, Bob is afraid of being rejected. So he has never tried to succeed at anything else, and he avoids taking risks where there are no guarantees. For Bob, it is better to stay in a predictable situation, however painful, than to go out and risk being shot down. By anyone. By anyone.

Bob experienced a lot of rejection in his early years. He never did well in school and rarely tried new things. In sports, Bob was the last to be picked for any team. When he asked women out, they laughed at him before rejecting him. He had low grades in school, and that carried over into almost every aspect of his life.

Over the years, Bob developed a "rejection complex" in his relationship with the world. So one day he decides that he doesn't want to be rejected anymore. One day, Bob simply decides that he has had enough. He wants to live differently. He wants to be the person he dreamed of being as a kid: passionate, excited, and ready to take on the world.

So, Bob does something completely irrational, unexpected, and totally unplanned. The turning point comes when a friend of his finally intervenes and says, "You are afraid because you create your own fear. You are unhappy because you choose to be unhappy. You fail because you believe in failure."

Next, **Bob makes an actionable decision**: Bob decides

that one day he will choose himself above all else, regardless of what other people think of him. He decides that instead of running away from his fear, he will embrace it and use it as an opportunity to learn. Instead of playing it safe and risking nothing, he will take a chance on anything that challenges him, even if it means looking stupid.

Recognizing how he has created his own misery by buying into his "rejection persona," Bob goes out into the world. He is afraid at first, but he takes action. He meets new people. He takes control of his life in ways he never dreamed possible, instead of letting life control him.

If he's not good at certain sports, he finds a sport he's good at and excels at it. If there are certain women who laugh at him or don't think he's good enough, he finds the woman of his dreams and just says, "To hell with the rest."

When Bob can't get into a university because of his low grades in school, he doesn't just settle for a low-paying, minimum-wage job; he teaches himself new skills and creates his own work online, selling courses and doing what he loves.

Now, when Bob faces rejection, he turns it into a positive experience by not buying into the expectations he once imagined the world had for him. In this way, Bob forges his own future. In time, he makes a new group of friends who support his endeavors, and he supports theirs.

Bob has changed. He is finally free.

Unlike Bob, most people who still live in fear of what they can't do are trapped in a cycle of rejection that they live to regret.

But how does Bob do it? He doesn't let the world tell him what he's worth. He laughs at people when they say he's crazy for trying something they wouldn't normally do. He does what others say can't be done.

Bob has a mission that he is very clear about: "Do the

things you've only dreamed of doing, and when you're done, do more of them."

Yes, Bob has fear, but he also has something else: conviction. He knows what he wants. He is working hard to get it. Despite the obstacles, he has made a decision to go through with it and keep going. Bob knows many people who have given up and accepted their fate as it was handed to them.

Bob isn't like that. Now he can't just lie down on the tracks and wait for the inevitable train to come and take care of his misery.

Bob is now a man of action. He does it, even in the face of fear. He takes his rejection on the chin and risks more. He has become immune to it. He asks for the things he wants, even when he is told NO. He is done trying to please other people and instead lives to make himself happy.

The more he succeeds, the more contagious his happiness becomes; he makes it his mission to share it with others. He doesn't just make a difference in his own life - everyone around him who comes into contact with Bob wants a piece of what he has.

Bob focuses on his dreams and creates a plan - a strategy - to get there. Some people hate Bob; he doesn't do things the way they're supposed to be done, and he doesn't care much about meeting their expectations of him.

He no longer cares about the haters of the world; he doesn't listen to their opinions, good or bad. Bob is free. He still has fear, but it is a tiny amount compared to the old Bob.

Now it's your turn...

Before we go any further, take thirty minutes to create your own "rejection-free persona" of the person you want to be. This doesn't mean that you have to change yourself in any way. What we do is ask ourselves a question: "If I could act differently in a way that would have a positive impact on my life, what would I do? How would I behave? What would I do differently?"

At this point, you may ask, "Where do I begin? How do I begin this journey to freedom? What is wrong with me that I am so afraid?"

In my experience dealing with rejection issues and situations, I have come to two conclusions:

The first is that we trap ourselves. We make judgments, formulate opinions, and meet expectations that lead to more of the same. When we buy into rejection, it solidifies the lies we formulated long ago about our personal worth and self-worth.

In a sense, we are all like Bob: afraid. We are afraid of what the world will think; we are reluctant to put ourselves out there because people will see us for the false persona we have tried so hard to hide.

This is the basis of self-rejection. We are harder on ourselves than anyone else. Staying hidden and out of sight is no way to live your life. It's certainly not going to put you on the path to fulfilling your master purpose or dream.

It is a continuous path to self-defeat. In our attempt to defuse the rejection of ourselves, we only create more of what we fear.

How many times have you made a decision based on the desire to make someone else happy?

This is a failed system that only creates unhappiness and an unfulfilled life. We make choices-not for ourselves, but for our parents, lovers, partners, and employers. You may say, "As long as they are happy, I am happy. When others are happy, we feel good. But you must also take care of your own happiness.

Are you willing to make a choice?

Bob represents a level of freedom that is available to everyone. If someone disapproves of something he does because it disrupts his schedule, Bob can live with it just fine. Bob has everything he ever wanted, and not because he had a great education or was popular. No, Bob has everything he wants because he knew what he wanted and made a clear plan for getting it. Bob freed himself by changing his attitude about himself.

> *When you shift the attitude and thinking you have about who you are, you care less about what others are judging you for.*

Bob made a decision that he would remove every obstacle between him and what he wanted. Bob's plan didn't include working all day in an office for someone else, surrounded by people he didn't like, doing a job he didn't like. Bob had bigger plans. Some people laughed at him. Some helped him.

The people who were there for Bob are his true friends. When you choose your own happiness over pleasing others just to get approval, you see who your true friends are. Then you can focus on pleasing the people in your life who care about you.

This is not to say that we can just do whatever we want without regard for others; it's about being who you want to be by choice, without fear of being pushed aside or stepped on. When we experience rejection in any form, we are most often rejecting ourselves before anyone else has a chance.

This is about choosing the person you want to be, not molding yourself into what others think you should be. We can all have what we want if we can only find the courage to break through the fear that keeps us from doing the things we love.

This is the second realization: **You are what you choose to**

be in every moment. You choose your actions, your thoughts, and your direction in life.

Be prepared for resistance. This mindset goes against how others perceive you and want you to behave. To break free, you must free yourself from the expectations of others.

As we will see in a later chapter, **asking for the things we really want is a powerful technique that can be mastered with practice**. By asking, you open up the possibilities of what is available.

When you face your fears and take action, amazing things begin to happen. You will find that there is a big difference between living in fear and living with fear. When we live in fear of rejection, we develop a "run and hide" attitude; it is easier to run from it than to face it.

The other option is to embrace what you are afraid of and develop a thick skin that can handle any kind of rejection. What we will learn is to find that balance between conformity and delinquency.

One of the core lessons we will cover is that you can choose yourself above all else

How much are you willing to sacrifice before you realize that when you accept any situation as something you have no control over, you give up that control and put yourself in the role of someone who is powerless?

The moment you decide that you have had enough of living in fear of being rejected, the changes in your life will begin.

This course is not a cure for rejection; it is a tool for dealing with it. There will always be situations and people who say NO. This is a fact of life no matter who you are.

What we are concerned with here is how you take the

rejection. Are you going to crawl under a rock and never go near rejection again or are you going to take the rejection you experience and use it to your advantage?

"Effort only fully releases its reward after a person refuses to quit."

—Napoleon Hill

3

Defeating Your Rejection Persona

*"No one can make you feel inferior
without your consent."*

—Eleanor Roosevelt

I would like you to consider the possibility that the rejection you have experienced is largely a product of your own creation. When we label ourselves as "rejected" or devalue our own self-worth because someone else has chosen NOT to accept us, we give up a great deal of our personal power. In other words, you are allowing someone else to determine if you are good enough.

If you're rejected for whatever reason, it's because the timing just wasn't right. The person you asked didn't need your services at that time, or the situation didn't work to their advantage because they have specific needs that you can't meet at that time.

This is a hidden opportunity. By being rejected, you can walk away with an opportunity to make yourself better for the next time. Let's get out of the habit of looking at this as a failure or thinking negatively, "See, I knew I was no good.

Now, imagine this scenario:

You are on your way to a job interview. As you enter the building and are asked to sit down, you notice the other candidates in the room. There are ten of them, five women and five men. They are all dressed in new suits and are as professional as you've ever seen them. Your mind immediately begins to undermine your confidence. You begin to compare yourself to these people and wonder if you are really supposed to be here.

Self-doubt begins to play with your mind. You begin to ask yourself questions that challenge your confidence:

- "I don't have enough education or experience."
- "These people are so much younger, more sophisticated, and look more determined than me."
- "What if I screw up? That'll just prove I'm a failure."
- "What if they ask me a question and I freeze up?"
- "What if it's a technical question because I'm really not good at technical things?"
- "What was I thinking coming here in the first place?"

This is how the road to self-rejection begins. I know - it could happen to anyone. You get nervous and you freeze up. You panic and have your moments of self-doubt. This is natural.

For the self-rejection persona, it is a daily pattern of self-defeat. You kill your chances before you have a chance to prove what you can do.

This is how you stay trapped - not by what the world does to you, but by what you do to yourself. If you can begin to recognize the pattern's of defeat and the negative thought process that begins to tear at your confidence, then you can formulate a better plan to deal with it. When you recognize your role in this, you become the "director" of your choices instead of just an actor on the stage.

One of the first steps in freeing yourself is to take responsibility for the rejection you create without anyone else's help.

Increasing Responsibility

Every choice you have made has brought you to this moment in your life. When you take responsibility for your current situation, just as it is, you become empowered by accepting your role in creating the situations you end up resenting. By recognizing that you are in control of your life and not everyone else, you move from a self-imposed victim state ("I have been rejected") to a state of deeper personal power ("Rejected? Me? Not so!").

The message I share with you in this book is this:

> The amount of fear you experience from rejection is directly proportional to the power you give it. You give people permission to reject you. This has nothing to do with the other side; it is your own choice. If you believe your rejection is real, it is. It will repeat itself throughout your life as a destructive cycle.

Two people can have the same experience and feel completely different. One person accepts what is happening as part of their growth and personal development; they have chosen themselves over the perceived rejection.

If you do not choose your life, you are rejecting it. When you reject it, you hand over the reins to these other people and let them make your choices for you. Giving up your right to live as a free individual is a form of self-rejection.

If living a life of feeling unworthy and inadequate is a prison, then liberating yourself by choosing who you are and how you want to live is the way to freedom. This is the goal: to choose yourself above all else and to reject the limitations you have imposed on yourself.

You must make clear choices about who you want to be. If you do not, someone else will make those choices for you.

If you don't make choices about your own life, rest assured that someone else will make the choice for you. You can only be free when you exercise your right to choose your actions.

It is a huge step when you can let go of self-judging condemnation. By silencing the inner critic that gets the "rejection" ball rolling, you can win the war instead of fighting your daily battles and exhausting yourself in the process.

If you are not in charge of your life, who is? If you cannot choose how you want to feel and have no control over your own feelings or emotions, then who does? If your emotions and thoughts are not created and controlled by you, then who is the creator? Asking these questions will give you the answers you seek.

It starts with taking responsibility for your life. I know this is a tall order. But playing the role of "victim" and expecting someone else to carry you is not a healthy option - especially if your goal is to break the cycle of rejection.

Remember this: **You are not rejected unless you give others permission to be**.

What I want you to consider is how much of your rejection is actually self-rejection? How much of your self-rejection is your ego? What thoughts are you tuning into when this happens? It's like the job interview example I gave you. You can be sitting alone in a quiet room with people around you and no one engaging in conversation and suddenly your mind is having a two-way conversation with your fear.

You can control your thoughts. No one has a mind control device that manipulates your thought patterns. So much of our suffering is self-inflicted. Responsibility isn't just a choice, it's a conscious action. You take control the moment you realize you have control.

Observe the communication you have in your own mind.

This is the "anonymous committee" that shows up when you are struggling with a situation and tries to give you advice.

When you reject this advice, it gets nasty and starts hurling insults:

- "You just don't have what it takes..."
- "You were rejected because you have no skills..."
- "If only you weren't so overweight..."
- "You see? I knew you'd mess up..."
- "Why don't you quit while you're ahead?"

You've probably heard these voices before. They are your inner critics, the dark side of your past struggling to survive in a world you never really learned to fit into. When you reject yourself, you create a "tunnel vision" mindset where every thought you create follows the direction of the one before it.

One dismissal leads to another; each negative blow to your character folds into a more powerful blow. Your pattern of self-debasement escalates.

It is a chronic mental habit that fuels the deep conviction that:

- You're not worth it.
- You don't matter.
- Your opinions and thoughts are useless.
- No one wants to know you.
- You should just give up.

To free yourself, you have to take control of the thoughts that are killing your mind. Our bad thoughts running amok are on autopilot, which means you can switch over and take full control of your flight path.

When you question the reasoning behind these automatic and negative thoughts, you'll see that they are connected to your past programming. And that programming can be overwritten and replaced with positive self-talk.

> *"Two men look out the same prison bars;*
> *One sees mud and the other stars."*

You can start today, right now, by refusing to be a victim of rejection, by saying "No more!" to the ideas, beliefs and thoughts that hold you captive and add to your fear. Take responsibility and start working on this now.

Stop the Blame Game

We have a habit of blaming ourselves when things don't go right. When our parents criticized us, we blamed ourselves for not being good enough.

When we were compared to others and told we didn't measure up, we looked down on who we were. When those closest to us told us we were unlovable, we believed there was something wrong with us. The words hurt, and so did the feeling of being abandoned, unwanted, and isolated.

- If only I could be better or try harder.
- If only I could do things as well as everyone else.
- If only I were somehow different.

Years later, no matter how hard we try to move past these negative feelings, they still linger. We have to become aware of what our emotions are trying to tell us. You need to question the feelings you have, especially if those feelings are hurting you.

Consider this question: "How can I choose myself when I have spent so many years rejecting who I am?"

When you get that rejection letter from the job you applied for, did they reject you? Or did someone else just have a better skill set than you? How many other people have been turned down for the same job?

When you ask someone out on a date and they say no, are they rejecting you or are you just not their type? Have you been rejected by every person you have ever approached?

When I analyzed all the situations in which I was afraid of being rejected, I came to a conclusion: When I thought about it rationally, I realized that people have preferences. I do not always fit into those preferences. There is no rejection here or anything to suspect. It is just the way it is.

When we are super sensitive about our rejection issues, it feels like everyone is out to reject us.

In reality, it could be that they just want something different at this time, and it could be that you don't meet those criteria. What we think of as rejection is actually a special form of "self-preference."

"Highly successful leaders ignore conventional wisdom and take chances. Their stories inevitably include a defining moment or key decision when they took a significant risk and thereby experienced a breakthrough."

—Larry Osbourne

4

Self-Rejection and Those Old Voices

"The effects of rejection can either kill your muse or change your life."

—Jane Champagne

We often make choices that lead to mediocre results. Instead of choosing the things we really want, we settle for what is available. We also settle for what we think we're worth, and for many people with rejection issues, that sense of worth is not very high.

Instead of choosing what is most important to us, we choose to settle for what is most important to other people. Instead of rocking the boat and taking charge of our lives, we drift and take life as it comes. And what we end up with is an outcome determined by someone else's needs instead of our own.

Before a job interview, I would think of all the reasons why they would probably reject my application. I would visualize myself failing and stumbling over my words. I imagined the interviewer asking a question and me not having the answer. I doubted my abilities and my ability to articulate my thoughts clearly. I was preparing myself to fall before I fell.

How many times do you allow yourself to be rejected by your own hand before anyone else has a chance?

It comes from accepting old beliefs that were recorded in our minds a long time ago. Being told we were no good, being ignored or not chosen, being told NO because we just couldn't cut it or didn't have what it takes.

The voices of the past, even though they are in the distant past, still have power over us

You must reclaim your power by making new choices that matter and that give you the upper hand in the game instead of playing by their rules. These are the choices that empower your goals to move you from a position of powerlessness ("I'll settle for whatever you give me") to a position of power and choice ("This is what I want and I won't settle for anything else").

You do this by choosing yourself first in everything you do

Rejection has taught us many things. It has taught us that self-doubt comes first from within. Others can doubt you (and they will), but it is you who doubt yourself the most.

Others can lack confidence in your abilities, but if you accept their perceptions as the only truth, you'll lose confidence in yourself. However, if you have already built up your confidence and you look at your life from a position of confidence, no one can take that away from you.

A mentor of mine, who was an excellent salesman, once told me about these rejection seminars in his industry that were designed to toughen people up for being told no. He said that some salespeople couldn't get over the rejection that came with

Self-rejection And Those Old Voices 31

the job. They took it personally when a customer didn't buy, as if their sales tactics were flawed.

But the ones who made it would just say, "Okay, who's next?" The seminar would focus on the psychological impact of being rejected by customers. And breaking it down so that the salesperson does not take the no personally. It is just a fact. No matter how good you are, there will always be someone who doesn't need what you have to offer.

For every 100 no's, you would get 1 yes. People don't necessarily buy from you because you're a nice person; they buy for their own reasons. If they say no, it's probably because they don't really need what you're offering.

But no one says no forever. Eventually someone will say YES, and then it becomes a numbers game. The salespeople who got frustrated and gave up after the first few weeks took it too personally because they identified themselves as the cause of the no's.

Life works the same way. Some will say YES and some will say NO. You'll be accepted by some and rejected by many more. People who free themselves from their habitual negative thinking can handle the judgments and words of their critics. After all, who really has the power to judge and condemn?

Most people I meet think they are always right in their opinions. In almost every case, our judgments are wrong. When people judge you, do they really know who you are? Can they look into your heart and make this observation with accuracy? Are they qualified to assign blame or tear apart someone's reputation?

Hopefully, as we move deeper into this book, you will feel yourself opening up to the possibility that rejection is largely a state of mind.

Better yet, as you come to accept that you are the one with

your finger on the button of change in your life, it becomes more about taking the initiative for and by yourself.

You have permission to put your self-worth first instead of believing you need someone else's approval. You have permission to hold yourself in the highest esteem without needing to be validated by rewards or promotions.

You can be yourself without someone else telling you who you should be based on their own opinions.

"There comes a moment that defines winning from losing. The true warrior understands and seizes the moment by giving an effort so intensive and so intuitive that it could be called one from the heart."

—Pat Riley

5

Redefining Your Personal Value

"After rejection–misery, then thoughts of revenge, and finally, oh well, another try elsewhere."

—Mason Cooley

My mentor once asked me, *"If you were to place a value on your self-esteem, what would it be?"*

I didn't understand the question. How can you put a value on self-esteem? Or confidence? I was thinking in terms of dollars and cents, so in a sarcastic attempt to be funny, I said, "A few dollars, I guess. Do you want to buy it?"

He said yes, took out his wallet and put five dollars on the table. He wasn't kidding either. Then he said, "I just bought your self-esteem. Now how does it feel?"

My mentor always had a point with his craziness, even if it sometimes came as "tough love," but the lesson was solid:

- Your self-esteem has value, just like your confidence.
- The amount of value is up to each of us and no one else.

But can you remember a time when you accepted the minimum price for something you valued? Maybe it was a garage sale and you'd just sold your favorite childhood toy for a few dollars because you really needed the money. You knew it was worth more, but you let it go anyway.

So, let me ask you this: *How much are you worth? What price do you put on your own value? How much is your time or your best idea worth?*

These are things that do not have a price tag. You can choose the value of your importance, but no one else can.

So why do people make choices that are really limitations in disguise?

We complain about our wages - but didn't you take the job knowing how much it would pay? We complain about having no time, yet we spend hours a day watching television. Isn't your time more valuable than watching TV, instead of working on a project that has the potential to change your life? We complain about the people who drive us crazy, but do we not choose to have them in our lives?

When you decide to choose yourself, you are making clear choices about the course of action you are taking, even if that action is to do nothing. When you meditate or think deeply about something, you don't move your body very much, but these actions still add value to your life. If you play video games all day or surf the Internet for junk sites, you are engaging in another type of activity that determines what your future will look like.

By choosing your actions today, you are choosing how you will live your life tomorrow. By choosing the kind of person you want to be, you are designing your life instead of just letting it happen.

When you choose yourself above the rest, it increases your confidence, eliminates fear, and kicks your rejection issues right out the door. The choices in the now are the choices of all your tomorrows combined.

We're so used to referring to the future as if it were something far away, when in fact it's the present moment and nothing more. That is all it has ever been.

You create your future by every choice you make in every present moment, which is the only place you really exist.

Choose wisely how you invest your time, emotional and physical energy. What do you want to learn? What courses can you take that will have a massive impact on your career and your contributions? What can you participate in that will reduce your fear and increase your ability to take positive action?

Choose your friends. Pick the people you want to spend time with. Who makes you feel so good that you want to spend all day or all week with them? On the other hand, who doesn't make you feel that way? Is there anyone who holds you back or pulls you into negative thinking?

We can't always choose the people around us (e.g., a coworker who shares an office with you, or a family member with whom you have friction). We can choose how we interact with them and what role we play in that person's world.

You can choose your salary instead of letting someone else dictate how much you get paid; you can choose the work you want to do instead of what you have to do for a paycheck. Did you choose your current job because you really wanted to do it, or are you just stuck there filling a chair? If so, why are you stuck? Did you choose to be stuck?

Remember that you can choose all of these things to make your life better, but by not choosing, you are also making another choice: to accept everything as it is and do nothing to improve your situation.

Choosing yourself first is about making firm choices. It is the ultimate decision and the most powerful choice you can make.

It is also not a one-time thing. I have to constantly remind myself in every situation that I am the one who makes the decisions.

No one else is going to give you a break. You can't count on someone else to go easy on you just because you have sensitivity issues.

Remember Bob? He cares, but he only cares about the things that are worth caring about.

If someone has a problem, it doesn't mean it has anything to do with you. Someone is in a bad mood? It's not your fault. Someone is unhappy about something you did, and they blame you? Take responsibility IF you think it's warranted, but don't just assume it's your fault.

People are often out of touch with their own reality and the scope of their feelings. They blame, scold, deny, judge, and move steadily toward a place of comfortable acceptance that makes them feel safe.

When you are criticized or judged, it is natural to take it personally. Someone doesn't like your work, your style, your clothes, your character, and so you think it's all about you and that you need to change something to gain their approval.

You hear it all the time: "If only they were more like this, I'd be happier."

If you had to change every time someone expressed an opinion or criticized you, you would be changing directions every ten minutes. Stay the course: Stay true to who you want to be, not who you think you should be.

The struggle with self-acceptance

Rejection always begins as an inside job. We reject ourselves 99% of the time by choosing not to choose who we are. If you try to please everyone, you'll end up giving someone else all the leverage and power to reject you even more.

To some extent, we are all a little self-conscious about what others think of us. We value an opinion, even if it's not always accurate. You might agree to something just to avoid a look of disapproval or to avoid disappointing someone, even if it means agreeing to something you didn't want in the first place.

We try very hard to be liked, accepted, and loved. We think that if we act in ways that people approve of, they'll think more highly of us. They'll invite us into their circle-until they find out we're faking it, and then we're kicked out.

My biggest fear when meeting someone new was: *"What if this person doesn't like me? What if they find out how weird or awkward or uncomfortable I am around people?"*

Everyone has different tastes, needs, and desires. As hard as it is to accept, not everyone wants what you have to give. Sometimes they will reject your skills ("You just don't have the skills for this job") or your love ("Sorry, you're not my type; I like short, stocky men"). They either want something or someone else. This is just a fact of life: we are selective creatures and make choices based on our own needs.

What you perceive as rejection is actually someone making choices based on their needs at the time. When you struggle with oversensitivity, any form of rejection becomes a personal barrier. You think it is you, when in fact it is the other person or the situation that is driving their choices at the time.

Because someone in your childhood convinced you that you were not worthy, those negative emotions and feelings and that hurt are still there. When you were criticized, you tried harder to please someone - a parent, a teacher, or someone close to you. But the criticism continued.

Someone took away your confidence, and now you want it back. This experience has created a state of hypersensitivity. When you are in a situation that challenges your self-esteem, you become extra sensitive as soon as that fear is tapped into.

Challenge Your Inner Skeptic

The skeptics and critics will always be there. They have nothing to do but target others who are trying to do something positive with their lives. They only have a say in what constitutes your personal worth if you give them permission, but you don't have to. You can keep it. You can choose. Set aside and schedule time during the day to really reflect on the emotions you are experiencing.

Stay in touch with the emotions, thoughts and feelings you are experiencing at any given moment. Tapping into your anxiety will indicate what needs to be addressed and dealt with. If you are procrastinating or resisting taking action, you are practicing "rejection avoidance" underneath the fear. This keeps the problem buried, but not solved.

Take time each day to observe your feelings. *How do you feel? What are you feeling? What are you afraid of? What can you do right now to deal with this situation?*

Writing down your feelings is an excellent way to bring them to your attention. Try starting each writing session with the words "I feel ..." and then writing whatever comes to mind. Write until you feel you have expressed everything you are feeling.

By putting yourself out there and challenging your fears of rejection, you open the floodgates to true personal empowerment

People with a rejection persona think they must be loved by everyone or hated by everyone. But the reality is that no one is loved or hated by everyone. It's not that simple. You're trying to be accepted by everyone, and sooner or later you're going to break your own value systems just to earn that acceptance.

Key Takeaway

In its negative mode, self-talk is like having someone standing behind you drilling you on all the things you do wrong. The inner critic is a tough teacher. Worse, we pass these negative thoughts on to our children and share our negativity with those around us.

When you are alone, listen to your self-talker. *What do you say to yourself? Are you using negative and demeaning put-downs?*

The person who is aware of their self-talk and can direct it has kicked the habit of rejection, and this will have a greater impact on their life.

"All forms of self-defeating behavior are unseen and unconscious, which is why their existence is denied."

—Vernon Howard

6

Breaking Free of the Predictable Path

"No matter what challenges you are faced with, or the opinions people have of you, rejection in and of itself from others is not a valid system to predict your future."

—Anonymous

When you avoid rejection, you eliminate the possibility of losing, looking bad, or failing altogether. You play it safe. You look for the fail-safe methods that are guaranteed to reduce your failure rate. Unfortunately, this way also reduces your success rate.

This is the path of predictability

Predictability works one of two ways: you either have a guarantee that it will work in your favor with a positive outcome, or you avoid the situation altogether for fear of failing or losing something of value.

Relying on predictability as a course of action creates a coping mechanism for dealing passively and aggressively with your deeper, unresolved issues.

The questions to ask yourself are:

- "What am I protecting?"

- "What am I afraid of losing?"
- "What do I risk not gaining if I avoid taking any risks at all?"

But the danger of creating a predictable life is that you choose routine over change; although routine serves us well in many ways, if you use it to avoid change as a means of escape, you are not moving toward freedom, but building bigger walls to fortify your personal prison. You are not truly free until you can face the fear of making real choices.

Do you know what happens when life is built on predictable choices? You avoid the difficulties and struggles that others face in order to eliminate the possibility of failure.

While this may eliminate your risk factor, by not taking any form of risk and not doing what your heart really wants, you end up feeding your rejection even more. You make it stronger. It thrives, and you fall deeper into the rabbit hole you were desperately trying to escape.

Rejectionism becomes more than a condition; it becomes a way of life. This way of life chooses the back road. You avoid the plateaus that lead to higher levels of growth. When life becomes a narrow highway, you make predictable choices that lead to obvious results.

Here is how you create a life of predictability that keeps you trapped:

- Avoiding talking to your spouse or partner about a problem for fear that they will not understand; instead, complaining to a friend about the situation
- Asking for $5 instead of $500 because you know you have a much better chance of getting less money.
- You ask for a date with someone who is an easy catch because the person you really want is out of your league,

while you fantasize about what it would be like to be with the person you really like;
- You don't try to change your current bad habits even though they are destructive and unproductive; you end up doing the same things over and over again because there's safety in what you know, even if it doesn't work very well.
- You stay in the same job you hate because everyone knows you and it's a steady paycheck; getting another job and starting over is risky if it doesn't work out.
- You don't make new friends because you prefer the company of old friends who already know you.

It comes down to risk. When you make decisions based on the risk factor, you set yourself up for success by getting what you ask for, but not what you really want.

This is what Steve Jobs meant when he said, "Don't settle."

Predictability is about taking second best. You ask for what you can get, not what you really value. Driven by feelings of shame and low self-esteem, a predictable lifestyle almost guarantees your success.

Make your own list of how you maintain a predictable lifestyle that actually keeps you trapped.

Now, I'm not saying that being predictable is a bad thing, because it's not. But if you are doing it to stay where you are for fear of moving forward, you are doing yourself a huge disservice.

Think of all the opportunities you are missing. The experiences you could be having right now if you did what you're afraid to do. The people you could connect with and the places you could go.

I stayed in the same job for fifteen years because I was afraid to apply for a new position. What if I didn't get the job? What if they questioned my training? What if I didn't have the skills or lacked something they needed?

I stayed in relationships that I resented and eventually hated because of my fear. I made excuses.

"Oh, we've been together a long time. It's too late to find someone else."

I avoided crowds and groups. I hated social events. People talk about themselves and their accomplishments - I had none to think about. I took no risks, so I had nothing to brag about. I didn't want people to question my background or find out the truth, that I was just ordinary, with no master's degree or awards to speak of.

I rarely made new friends. I stayed with the same people. It was more predictable and therefore safer. I am not saying there is anything wrong with having the same friends all your life - of course not. But do you try to meet new people? Are you afraid of social situations because of what they might say or do?

Our choices become pathways that support our rejectionism by controlling the outcome. There is little risk. Life is boring, but it's safe. We don't have to face the shame or humiliation that comes with rejection.

What is the solution? How do you break out of this life of predictability to start living? What will it feel like when you look back at the end of your life and see all the opportunities you gave up because you were afraid?

Breaking Your Predictable Paths

We choose the people, places, and situations that have the least chance of rejecting us.

It could be an old relationship or a job you've had for twenty years. You may not like your current situation, but you're sticking with it because you don't want to change. Be honest - change takes courage. Sometimes it takes discipline to find that courage.

Being predictable is all about avoiding change; and avoiding change is closely related to avoiding rejection. One of the main reasons we never get over rejected child syndrome is that we spend most of our lives hiding from it.

You can't recover if you're constantly on the run

So, the question you need to ask yourself is this:

"What do I have to lose?"

To break your predictability, you have to do the things you would not normally do. These are easy to identify. They're the actions you've always wanted to try on the inside, but haven't on the outside because you've already visualized the negative outcome. In other words, you won't do it because you're not willing to risk your humiliation or shame. Your rejection.

But you can. What is the worst thing that can happen?

You can break the predictable patterns that keep you stuck

Here are two steps to breaking predictability and putting yourself out there:

Step 1: Notice your daily habits

I took this step for a period of six months, during which I recorded my daily activities. This included not only the tasks I performed, but also the people I associated with, the places I visited, and even the food I ate. I discovered that my routine was the same every day. I even took the same route home every night.

By breaking up your routine, just making small changes here and there, you can begin to bring some uniqueness back into your lifestyle. When that happens, your risk appetite expands and you're ready to try new things.

Why is this important? You'll become comfortable taking risks, and when I say risks, I'm not talking about jumping between buildings, but realistic risks. Like meeting new people. Putting your voice out there. Getting over the fear of being judged or criticized.

Then try new things. Go to a different coffee shop where different people hang out. Get out of your comfort zone and into something new. It's natural to have a routine that we're used to, but is your routine keeping you in one place? I realized it was, and I wanted to make some changes that would get me to try new things.

Step 2: Put yourself in a situation where you will be rejected

I had a job interview a while back. It went well, even though I didn't get the job in the end. But I knew I wouldn't get it anyway. I did it on purpose because I wanted to desensitize myself to the fear of interviews. I've never been good at interviews, so I put myself in a position where I knew I'd be rejected.

It worked. After a few more interviews, I didn't care what they thought. I wasn't good enough for their company? There were plenty of other opportunities out there. I was going to look for them and take advantage of everything I could.

The funny thing is, the one company that I didn't think would hire me actually made me the offer. I didn't take the job, but I'm pretty sure the reason they offered me the position was because I was relaxed and confident during the interview. Sometimes it pays to just not care.

When you do something you wouldn't normally do, you're stepping out of your predictable comfort zone. Everyone has a comfort zone where they feel completely safe. It's like a protective cocoon. We need it for stability and to feel safe.

But if your comfort zone is designed to be a prison, consider changing old habits. It doesn't have to be an all-or-nothing maneuver. A single action-even a small step-can create a multitude of ripples.

Key takeaway

Think back to a time in your life when you took a risk and failed. Maybe you tried a new line of work or invested in something that lost you money. You asked someone out on a date and they said NO. You asked for money, but it was a fraction of what you really wanted. You passed on a business strategy because you were afraid it wouldn't work.

Put yourself in that position again and imagine what you would do differently if you had another chance. How would you talk to the person you want to meet? How much money would you ask for and how would you ask for it? What job would you go to interview for, knowing that you were the right person for the job?

To break out of your comfort trap, visualize it happening. You have to see yourself doing it. Run the scenario through your mind over and over again. Each time you do this, you make the vision stronger.

Visually and mentally see yourself taking the actions you really want to take. Try to do this for ten minutes a day. Spend time in the morning visualizing how your day will go if you do the things that are out of your comfort zone. You will begin to break the predictability trap and get closer to freeing yourself.

"You can search throughout the entire universe for someone who is more deserving of your love and affection than you are yourself, and that person is not to be found anywhere. You yourself, as much as anybody in the entire universe, deserve your love and affection."

—Buddha

7

Rejection and Love Dependency

"Remember that the best relationship is one in which your love for each other exceeds your need for each other."

—Dalai Lama

After spending most of our lives feeling unloved, ashamed, or humiliated, many of us have internalized the core belief that no one can possibly love us. We are convinced that we are destined to be alone, and that being alone is better than being rejected.

But when this happens, your love for others becomes clingy, desperate, and ultimately hurtful. Love becomes conditional rather than unconditional. You begin to love for survival instead of developing healthy relationships.

This fuels the belief that because you are unlovable, those closest to you will inevitably reject you. This in turn leads to love addiction or love despair: when you are so desperate for people to like you, it repels people.

You either try too hard to get others to accept you, which makes you seem needy and desperate, or you hold yourself back, afraid to put yourself out there for fear that your love will be thrown back at you. Putting yourself out there, telling people you care, is like walking on a ledge, afraid of falling off.

Experiencing rejection in relationships is a huge trap for

Rejection And Love Dependency

those with a Rejection Personality. You never really feel accepted or that your love is valued. Criticism and shame are at the forefront of every interaction.

Our relationships are largely based on trying to hide this rejection. But the more intimate a relationship becomes, the more impossible it is to maintain a false front. As soon as the other person realizes how desperate you are, or that you are not being completely transparent, the relationship ends.

The cycle then repeats itself in the next one. Vulnerability is not an emotion most of us are willing to risk, so we hide who we are from the people we want to love the most. In the end, it is a lose-lose situation.

In the relationship where rejection is an issue, love is something that is based on conditions. You are lovable if you are good; you are lovable if you follow the rules and do what you are told. You're lovable if you don't embarrass me at the party.

This reinforces the belief you formed in childhood that if you do what we say, you will be loved. Conditional love is always built on a foundation of conditions or requirements that must be met before you receive the love you so desperately crave. This comes from a critical parent or guardian when you were growing up.

Nothing you did was ever good enough, so you tried harder. When it seemed that absolutely nothing was good enough, you gave up and surrendered to the feeling of inadequacy. This is one of the origins of developing a rejection persona.

First of all, conditional love isn't real love. This kind of love falls under the guise of "I will love you IF you..."

To become worthy of another person's approval, you must somehow earn it. It is like going to work and getting paid. We will pay you this much IF you do the job we expect. Love isn't a condition. It is an absolute. It has to be, otherwise it becomes a negotiation.

If you have children, you know what this means. You love your children unconditionally. Yes, they misbehave and act up and do the things you don't want them to do. They may even get into real trouble at some point. But they are still your children. Unconditionally.

Now, in your daily life, most of the people you interact with will not love you unconditionally. You will be met with conditions in most situations in your life. People will like you if you do this or that; if you do a good job for your boss, you're on her good side; if you screw up, you're on her other side.

The rejection persona has become accustomed to this conditioned way of loving. But many people who crave love crave unconditional love. But because you're conditioned, you try to meet all the conditions that everyone puts on you in the hopes that you'll fulfill another person's desires and receive the unconditional acceptance you seek. It's a vicious cycle.

We spend most of our lives "seeking," looking for the things that are missing inside. We missed out on love as children, and now we want someone else to give it to us. Our parents didn't give us the love we should have received, and now there is a big hole in our lives where love should be.

The dilemma is that if you look for it "out there," you'll spend the rest of your life trying to fill that big hole. The outside world cannot give you anything that is lasting or permanent.

You have never been accepted or recognized for anything of value, so you feel worthless. As a result, you seek acceptance and value from others. And how much more do you need before you feel completely fulfilled? It's like a bottomless pit, and no amount of encouragement or positive reinforcement anyone can give you will ever be good enough.

When you spend your life seeking and expecting some form of payback, you want what is owed to you: love, love, and more love. As a child you were devalued and undervalued. Your grades in school were never good enough, you were bad at sports, or you always seemed to be "in the way" at home.

It is painful to accept, but if you do the deep analysis work and come to terms with your rejection persona in relationships, you will come to this conclusion: The love you are trying to find and extract from your relationships will never be enough.

It's not the same, not the way your parents could have given it to you. You will only become frustrated and begin to reject or put down your partner as a means of defending your position in the relationship. Power struggles will erupt and the relationship will take a bad turn.

Rejected people struggle with unconditional love most of their lives. If you didn't receive it as a child, you will spend the rest of your life trying to get it from people who may be unwilling or unable to give it to you.

This puts a lot of pressure on the person you have only been dating for a few weeks, and you want to be loved as no one has ever loved you before. When this person rejects your demands, you become needy and desperate. Picking up on this hungry dependency, the other person will flee the relationship.

People with dependency issues are looking for unconditional love in all the wrong places. We've established that. So, the question becomes:

"Where can I find this unconditional love?"

Just as you must first choose yourself in order to build trust, reliability and confidence, you must first love yourself. Asking the world to give you this love is unrealistic. You will fail if you have these expectations of others.

Of course, we all need and desire love from other people, but relying completely on another person to fill the missing part of your life will lead to emotional setback and eventual disappointment. But if we treat the people we come into contact with every day with respect, admiration, and appreciation, they will pick up on your positive attitude toward them.

As the Dalai Lama has wisely said: *"If you want others to be happy, practice compassion. If you want to be happy, practice compassion."*

I have found no better way to create unconditional love than to give the best of myself at all times. I know this sounds like a tall order, and it's not always easy to accept everyone, but try to open your mind and heart as much as you can.

Instead of desperately searching for the love you feel is missing, turn it around and realize that you have everything you need: It just needs to be nurtured.

The one obstacle that holds people back is putting themselves in a position of vulnerability. We are afraid to just put ourselves out there in case we get hurt or taken advantage of. But protecting ourselves is what we have been doing for a long time, and even though it feels natural and necessary to move away from that rejection, by letting go of that fear of vulnerability, you reduce the pain of going through a rejection.

How to Practice Unconditional Love

Want to experience unconditional love? Treat people unconditionally. Do things for them without expecting anything in return. Say nice things about them and don't ask for anything in return. The moment you do something for someone and attach a desire or expectation to it, you are building up disappointment. Successful relationships are built on four important values:

- Mutual respect
- Appreciating the people you are with

- Avoidance of any form of harsh criticism
- Giving without high expectations

Relationships based on a give-and-take strategy don't experience the unconditional love that could be fostered by practicing these four simple principles.

But the "I'll love you if you love me" approach - in any relationship, not just romantic - sets you up for failure.

As soon as one person decides they don't want to share that love, it's gone. Your unconditional love pact is over. You have to wake up to this truth if you are going to get over this massive hurdle. It's time to accept that the unconditional love you should have had as a child is most likely not going to happen.

One lesson I have learned from being in several dependent relationships is this: You can't get anything from someone if they're not willing or able to share. No one can give you what he or she doesn't have. And the fact is, relying on someone to meet all your needs isn't going to work in the end.

If you have really deep issues around codependency, you may need a big push to get yourself to take action. You won't be lovable until you learn to give it away

The cure isn't complicated - look at how you interact in relationships and take a moment to tap into your feelings. Are you being genuine or putting up a front? Are you being completely open, or do you feel like you're hiding your true self for fear of being exposed? Are you interested in this relationship for its potential, or is there an underlying motive?

Unconditional love is getting to the place where you can accept yourself completely, without illusions of perfectionism or feeding the needy desires of a childhood ego. Unconditional love isn't what you have to have for everyone, but it is what you need for yourself and your children.

Many of our rejection-persona issues come from childhood. They started there, and it is too late to go back and fix what was done. But you can begin to move forward today.

Focus on loving yourself in a way you never were as a child. Revisit your childhood and relive those feelings of shame, guilt, and rejection.

Reach out to yourself and give the love that was withheld. Visualize yourself wanting these things as a child and not getting them. Walk yourself through the pain of those moments.

Pull yourself back in when you try to escape. Focus on that memory and let it happen. See yourself wanting this approval and being rejected for it.

Tapping into these memories brings up painful emotions. But these are the feelings you have been escaping for most of your life.

By avoiding what happened, you keep the lies that built this false persona. Uncovering the truth and fully realizing that it was not your fault frees you from this pain over time.

Key takeaway

Look for areas in your life where you expect love but aren't getting it. Is it from your wife, husband, partner or lover? How about your children? Do you have unrealistic expectations? Are you needy or do you come across as demanding for love?

Focus on giving your love to someone in a way that you have never received it. I don't mean romantic love, but genuine caring for other people. Because rejection is such a deep and painful issue, most people don't want to admit or even recognize that they have it. But you do. Everyone does to some degree, some more than others.

By helping others, you create the opportunity to increase your personal worth. I have found that by helping others, I have naturally developed a deeper love for myself that was never there before. Believe me, if you like and respect yourself, you'll never have to worry about a lack of love in your life.

If there is anything that can remove the fear of rejection, it is putting yourself out there, loving yourself more, and truly accepting the kindness of others. There are a lot of people out there who need people like you. Don't let the "rejection bug" stop you from giving.

Make a list of the things you are ashamed or embarrassed about.

Is it...

- Being alone?
- Being jealous or envious of others?
- Wanting to be someone else instead of who you could be?

Walk through your emotions and observe how you feel. If we can identify the situations that trigger rejection, we are in a better position to take action.

By knowing when you are experiencing a "rejection moment," you can put an end to this vicious cycle.

PART 2

JUST ASK FOR IT!

8

Why We Fear Asking

*"Rejection doesn't have to mean you aren't good enough;
it often just means the other person failed to notice
what you have to offer."*

—Ash Sweeney

Asking for what we want most is one of the hardest things to do. We fear hearing that word NO more than any other word in the language.

Think back to when you were a child. You probably asked for everything you could get. When you didn't get it, you became persistent and demanded it.

If your parents said no (which they often did), you'd go away for a while, but return later with a new plan of attack. You probably resorted to negotiating - "I'll clean my room for a week if you let me have what I want."

Eventually you either got what you wanted or you finally conceded that you had lost. You would pursue every avenue until what you wanted - the new toy or the latest cool gadget— was yours.

But over the years, we change

We start asking for less and end up taking what is available. We lose the hard bargaining and whining that worked for us as children. Our parents often told us to stop whining or being selfish, so we did. After all, no one wants to be labeled as selfish.

This brings us to the power of asking, one of the core themes of this book and a primary obstacle to facing rejection.

The fear of being rejected is what keeps a rejectee from taking any kind of action. Instead of demanding or even asking, we tend toward acceptance and passive numbness. This is a path that leads to suffering.

We suffer when we go without while we watch others get what they want because they asked for it. You may develop resentment, not only toward those who are "braver" than you, but you'll label yourself as weak and a coward.

When you have to give up something because you don't have the courage to ask for it - when we give up the things we want because we know we could have them if we just stood up and did something - it hurts.

We buy into our own rejection and actually create more of it. You may avoid conflict or rejection by not asking, thinking you will be spared the emotional pain of hearing NO, but the consequences are far worse in the long run.

In their groundbreaking and bestselling book, *The Aladdin Factor*, authors Jack Canfield and Mark Victor Hansen (Chicken Soup for the Soul) tell us that nothing comes without first deciding that you deserve it, want it, and will have it. Then, knowing these facts, you seek out the right people to help you get it.

In this section, we are going to discuss exactly that: **how to make a decision based on what you want, and then figure out your plan for getting it.**

Asking for the things you want is one of the best strategies and habits for developing personal freedom. When you take a risk by asking for something, you open huge doors for yourself.

Opportunity doesn't come knocking and look for takers;

we have to make the opportunity by stepping up, saying YES, and taking direct action. Asking is the key to taking charge of your life and the success that follows.

The bottom line: **If you don't ask, you don't get**.

Here are some reasons why we don't ask:

- The answer will be a resounding NO (so why bother).
- You will be embarrassed or humiliated if you are turned down.
- You fear that if they say YES, you'll be expected to return the favor.
- We undermine our own self-confidence by believing that we are not worthy of receiving it.
- Pride gets in the way when we associate asking with begging.
- Low self-esteem issues: my needs are not that important and I can do without.
- I might be judged as poor because I don't already have it.

When you ask for something you want, your confidence skyrockets and you prove to yourself that the fear you had was just an illusion keeping you trapped.

When you ask, you desensitize your fear of rejection. We will discuss desensitization more in the next section, but for now, know that developing the habit of asking is the key to eliminating the fear of rejection.

For years, I was too passive. I expected things to just come my way, or that people would figure out what I wanted and give it to me without my asking.

But no one knows better than you what you want. People cannot read your mind. If you wait for someone to figure out what you want and then hope that they give it to you, you could be in for a long wait and a great deal of disappointment.

That's not patience; it's a form of self-denial

If you knew all you had to do was ask, you could have everything you've ever wanted. But many people don't have what they want, and they go without because they didn't ask for it.

Why is that? We believe the answer is NO. And when we hear that word NO, it takes us back to our childhood when we were denied the things we really wanted. Who denied us? Parents, teachers and peers.

How many times have you been told, "Don't ask for it because you won't get it"? Fair enough - but still, we didn't get it; the want is still there. I can still remember things I wanted in my childhood that I never got. Can you?

It sounds like such a simple concept. You ask for things all the time, right? But it's not the frequency of asking that matters. You have to ask for the right things.

If you ask for the wrong things all your life, any request will do. Why ask for oranges when you want apples? In other words, stop asking for things you don't want or need.

There are three truths about asking:

1. People who ask for what they want are usually rejected.
2. People who don't ask for what they want never get rejected because they never ask.
3. People who keep asking for what they want may get rejected, but eventually they'll get what they want.

I came to the conclusion that I could keep getting what I have always gotten. Or I could push myself to try to get the things I never imagined I could get. When you ask for what you want instead of what you think you're worth, it's like putting the key in the right lock: You open up a whole new world of possibilities.

It follows a simple philosophy:

- Ask and you may receive.
- Don't ask and you will never receive.

When I started asking for things, everything changed. I got some NOs; but I also got some people who said YES. And my averages were good. I got a YES about 60% of the time. If I hadn't asked for anything, I wouldn't have gotten anything. 60% works better than 0%.

Asking is the key to success. This is especially true when it comes to asking for help. I'll talk more about that later.

For years I lived in procrastination because I was afraid the answer would confirm what I already believed: I wasn't worth it, and that's why I was always rejected.

This "asking action" changed the way I thought about overcoming my rejection addiction. For most of my life, I was afraid to ask for anything. I didn't want to get in the way or bother anyone.

In other words, I didn't want to put myself in a position where I risked being rejected. If they said NO - and that was a very real possibility - it would reinforce every belief I had about myself that I was unworthy of getting the things I really wanted.

How do you know you can have something if you never ask for it? By asking for what you want, you increase your chances of getting it exponentially.

If you don't ask for it, your chances of getting nothing are almost guaranteed. No one can read your mind; they don't know what you want, and even if they did, would they just offer it to you? Most likely not.

Years ago, I stopped asking for what I wanted for fear of opening myself up to vulnerability, owing someone something I could never repay, or being seen as weak or needy. My pride would get in the way.

There are so many things I have wanted in my life that I have never received for one reason. It wasn't a lack of money or ability; it was a lack of courage to ask for what I wanted most.

Not asking for what you want for fear of looking stupid, feeling powerless, being humiliated - these are all fears of rejection. You learned at a young age that it is better to take what you can get than to risk everything by asking for what you want. You don't want to seem needy or helpless.

There is a price to pay for not asking. You may avoid the humiliation of being rejected, but by avoiding asking for what you really want, you lose much more.

By trading your pride and fear of embarrassment, you could be giving up large sums of money (asking for a raise), your freedom (asking for time off), and the opportunity to thrive instead of survive.

Here is a list of reasons why asking is important:

- If you don't ask for directions, you'll end up going the wrong way.
- If you don't ask for financial help to go back to school, you won't get a good education and you'll end up unemployed, possibly permanently.
- If you don't ask to borrow someone else's car because yours broke down and you need to get to work, you'll miss a day's pay and the manager won't be happy.
- If you don't ask that person out, someone else will.
- If you don't ask for more money at work, you'll have less money.
- If you don't ask for support, you'll end up doing it alone.
- If you don't ask how it's done, you'll end up doing it the wrong way

- If you don't ask for an extension, you'll be up late tonight trying to get it all done.
- If you don't ask for time off, you'll work harder and risk burning out.
- If you don't ask the waiter to heat up your food more because you want it hotter, you'll end up paying full price for an expensive meal that's cold.
- If you don't ask your spouse to listen to you when you have something important to say, you'll end up unfulfilled, unhappy, and resentful.
- If you don't ask for a second chance, you have to accept your first attempt as a painful lesson in failure.

By not asking, you are taking a huge risk. You are making a choice to be less, to have less, and ultimately to want less. You will eventually excuse yourself and say, "Oh, that's okay, I didn't really need it anyway.

Really?

You don't want help with something? You don't want more money for your hard work or more time off? You don't want more friends or people to listen to you? You don't want more confidence? You don't want a discount on your hotel room? You don't want to go out with the girl who lives down the street, even though she's been looking at you every morning as you jog by? You don't want a bank loan to buy a new house?

I don't think so.

And neither should you.

Selling yourself short is telling the world, "I'm not worthy of any of these things, so I'm not going to ask for anything." If that's the case, you're going to end up shortchanged. You'll get what others give you. And what they give you might be the remains of the good things they are done with.

If you don't ask for the things you really want, there's always someone else who will. While you are busy waiting for someone to give you what you secretly want, others are moving forward, asking and receiving their gifts.

The Risk Worth Taking

If you could ask for anything you wanted from this day forward, where would you start? What would you ask for first?

Make a list of all the things you have been holding back. Would you ask for help with a project? Would you go to the bank and ask for a loan to start that business? Would you ask for better benefits at work? Would you ask your friend or a stranger for help?

Make a list of all the things that would dramatically improve your situation. Here are some ideas:

- What would you ask for at home?
- What about when you are out in public? Would you ask someone to move their car so you could squeeze into the next parking space?
- What would you ask for in a restaurant? A coffee shop? A shopping mall?
- Would you ask for a discount on older items in a store?
- Would you ask a stranger for a cup of coffee?
- Would you ask someone to lend you money with the promise that you would pay it back within a certain period of time?
- Would you ask someone to treat you with more respect and stop criticizing you?

The power of asking is one of the key components to really kicking your fear of rejection out of your life. You can numb your fear by taking action and doing something every day that desensitizes you to that fear.

Asking is like taking a risk. But it is a good risk. It's the risk that gets you out of a rut and gives you more control over your life. You feel powerful and centered. By asking, you take control of your life. The fear of being rejected is reduced to a tiny whimper. Eventually you won't even feel it.

Now that is something worth having

If it's true that by asking you get what you ask for, you also deprive yourself of the things you don't ask for.

Don't ask and you won't get; ask once and you might get it. Ask again and again, and you'll increase your chances of getting something exponentially!

It's that simple.

At the very least, by asking for what you want and putting yourself out there, you'll build up a strong resistance to hearing NO. The more you hear NO, the easier it gets. You will desensitize yourself to being told to go away.

When you ask and someone looks at you with doubt and you know they won't do what you ask, instead of feeling that pang of fear that says, "Ouch, I've been told no again," you will develop a tougher skin for being told no. Instead of fearing rejection, you will come to embrace it.

In his best-selling novel *Rejection Proof*, author Jia Jiang put rejection to the test. For one hundred days, he put himself in situations where he asked for literally anything, often very absurd things that people would surely say NO to. Several times he was shocked to actually get a YES and the opportunity to try something he would never have thought of.

By putting himself in situations where he was almost

guaranteed to fail, he desensitized himself to being told no. After one hundred days, he had more freedom than he had ever experienced.

As Jiang learned through this experiment, you're not cured by being rejected once, but by being rejected all the time. It acts as a great confidence booster and pushes the power of rejection right out the door. We will discuss this more in Section 3, but as the rejection experiments have proven, you only earn your freedom and break these "chains" when you go out there and do it.

For years I did not ask for anything unless I absolutely had to. If it was something I needed and couldn't live without, and I was in a position where asking another person was the only way to get it, I would do it. But only under extreme circumstances.

I was like a silent watchdog, always keeping an eye on things I wanted, but staying in the shadows and watching while others moved forward by taking action.

For years I made excuses for not asking. I would say things like:

> *"I can figure it out on my own."*
> *"Oh no, don't bother. I'll take care of it."*
> *"It's not important."*
> *"I'll ask tomorrow."*

If this is you, let's take action to change it. Don't be a silent watchdog and suffer. You deserve to have everything you ever wanted. You deserve it no matter what your mind tells you.

"One of life's fundamental truths states, "Ask and you shall receive." As kids we get used to asking for things, but somehow, we lose this ability in adulthood. We come up with all sorts of excuses and reasons to avoid any possibility of criticism or rejection."

—Jack Canfield

9

Essentials to Asking for What You Want

"Everyone at some point in life have faced rejection and failure, it is part of the process to self-realization."

—Lailah Gifty Akita

Here are the eight steps you can use to ask for anything you want. It's going to be hard at first, but after you put yourself out there and do it, you'll get the hang of it.

Soon, you'll be asking for anything without feeling guilty.

Step 1: STOP thinking about the negative outcome of being rejected and hearing NO.

It doesn't matter because if you don't ask, you're rejecting yourself and you won't get anything anyway. You've created a lose-lose situation before you even start. Focusing on a bad outcome will affect the way you ask, if you ask at all.

If you expect to be rejected, you'll go into the situation with no confidence at all. People are much more likely to give you something if you act like you really deserve it. If you show fear or are already dreading the first NO, it will show. If you are focused on the outcome not being what you want, turn it around so that you are visualizing yourself getting the YES.

Step 2: Visualize the action of the ASK, not the response - it is not important that you get a YES.

Of course that's what you want, but if you put everything on getting the YES and you keep getting the NO, you'll go back to thinking about the negative outcome.

The positive outcome is the action of you asking. Not the result. You are so focused on the answer that you forget that the courage to ask in the first place is the real victory. Forget the result. Focus on the action of asking. You can do this by visualizing yourself doing it.

See yourself opening the door and walking into a room. The person standing between you and what you want is sitting in a chair in the middle of the room. Imagine walking right up to him or her and asking for the one thing you have always wanted. Now take it a step further and watch them react to your request.

You can run through different outcomes; would they get angry and start yelling, or would they smile and just say, "Sure, you can have it. Why didn't you ask me before?"

I used this technique a lot when I was struggling with asking. I still do. Visualizing yourself doing it is a powerful way to build your courage, and it actually gets you excited about doing it. You'll feel less fear and anxiety.

Step 3: Ask yourself, "What's the worst thing that could happen?"

Rejection is a game of deception. When you imagine yourself taking a risk or moving toward something that triggers fear, the feeling is like drowning. You think you won't survive and that death is imminent.

But let's be practical: What's the worst that could happen? You have to remind yourself that life goes on. You'll get through it. You have nothing to lose (except pride and ego), so why not? If you don't ask, you'll lose anyway.

We often attach a catastrophe to the outcome, as if a rejection is the end of everything. This fear is based on the belief that we can't handle it. "If they reject me, my life will be forfeit." I can tell you that life will go on, and the great thing is that you'll develop a mental toughness for it.

Step 4: Understand that rejection is an illusion

It is the ultimate lie that traps you. As long as you believe you have everything to lose, you will be paralyzed by fear of doing anything. I convince my subconscious that rejection doesn't exist, I accept it in my own mind.

Sure, we're going to be pushed aside, rejected, and told we're just not good enough. But this is the journey that successful people take. If you let one rejection stop you from persevering, you'll spend your entire life struggling to get anything done.

The power of illusion is as strong as you make it. You can let it defeat you, or you can accept it into your life as part of the growing process.

Step 5: Keep asking

Success is in the numbers: the more you ask, the better you get at it. It is a skill you can master with practice. You may only get one YES out of fifty rejections, but it's better than nothing. And nothing is what you'll get if you don't ask.

Remember that timing has a lot to do with your success rate. There have been times when I have asked people for something once and they said NO; but when I asked again, they agreed. Were they having a bad day when I asked the first time? Maybe they didn't need what I was offering at the time?

Persistence pays off. Believe in what you are asking for and ask with conviction. This will increase your chances of success.

Step 6: Know WHO to ask and stop complaining about not getting what you want

There's no point in asking an unemployed person for a job; they can't give you what they don't have. You must ask the right people. This means don't waste your time asking people who have nothing to do with what you want. Also, complaining to others about your hard luck and not having what you want will only perpetuate your situation of having less.

For a long time, I had a bad habit of complaining to friends and anyone who would listen about how I was always missing out. If someone I knew became successful because they took the initiative and went after their goals (most likely by asking a lot of questions), I would be consumed with jealousy and complain about how lucky he or she was. Luck had nothing to do with it.

Bottom line: stop complaining. You have no reason to complain and it can only do you more harm while building a wall of resentment. If you don't take action to get what you want, you have no one to blame but yourself.

Step 7: Know WHEN to ask

Your timing can have a lot to do with the outcome of your asking moment. You wouldn't want to ask someone for a favor when they're in the middle of a personal crisis. For one thing, they may not be able to help you at that moment, or there may be too much going on at that time. Observe and take notes. Know what you want to ask for and then watch for the right moment.

The most powerful approach is to do it with empathy. If possible, observe the situation and try to understand the other person's emotions and feelings at the time. This can be challenging in a business environment, but each situation has its own unique approach.

For example, asking your spouse for something would be different than asking a co-worker or manager. The level of empathy is also different, but by assessing the situation and approaching when the timing feels right, you can get a better result.

Step 8: Know WHAT to ask for

One of the biggest reasons people give up is because they don't know what they want. You need to be clear about what you want, or you'll end up asking for the wrong things; or worse, you'll just take what everyone else is giving away.

Remember: People usually don't want to give you what you want, especially if they want to keep it, or if what you're asking for will cost them something.

But knowing WHAT you want will also determine WHO you ask. On the list you made at the beginning of all the things you are going to ask for, now go back and write down the name or names of the people who can give it to you.

Who can you go to today? Is there one person above all others who can give you what you want? Then you know what to do. But you may have doubts. You think they'll reject you, or worse.

*"We cannot become what we need to be
by remaining what we are."*

—Max Depree

10

Simple Strategies for Asking

"Rejection can disappoint you, depress you and may even stop you in your tracks... learn not to take rejection so personally... if you're honest with yourself and believe in your work, others will too."

—Bev Jozwiak

Now, make a list of twenty things you are going to ask for today.

Who will you ask? When will you ask? How much will you ask for?

Be specific about what you want. Just asking for "time off" from work isn't specific enough. You need to ask for three days or three weeks. Make sure that what you ask for is what you really want and that it is specific.

When you go to the bank for a loan, you don't just say, "Give me some money for a car." You have to say how much you need.

Be specific.
Be clear.
Be confident.

Now, here are the nine strategies you can put into action when you ask:

1. Keep track of your asking score

Here is a tactic you can use when you are procrastinating. A friend of mine kept two jars: one full of pennies and one empty.

When he took a positive action, such as completing a simple task or asking for something, he would move a penny to the empty jar. It worked because this simple action of moving pennies prompted him to do something every day. He said he wanted to see how many pennies he could fill the empty jar with.

Make a challenge to yourself and start the month with two jars, one empty and one filled with thirty coins (or jelly beans or whatever you want). Then set a goal each day to ask for one thing you want. It doesn't have to be something extravagant.

Whether you get a YES or a NO, you still win. The victory is in getting to the "ask" stage. Beyond that, the result doesn't matter.

2. It's about giving and giving some more

When I learned to ask more and could confidently approach people about my desires to have, be, or do something, I had a great moment of clarity.

When I received, I didn't just want to get more and keep taking. That's not what asking is about. You have to be willing to give as much as you get and more. There will come a time in your life when people will ask you for the things you want.

I realized that I was willing to give what I had received; but when I was rejected, or when I rejected myself by holding on to my "ask," I was less willing and kind to share with others.

My rejectionism had created a level of scarcity in me that

made me unwilling to give. I was holding on and building a barrier around my life. Asking was another way to freedom, and it can be yours.

3. Believe you're worth receiving

For many years I was afraid to ask for what I wanted. The reason was that I didn't think I was worthy of having it. Lacking confidence and low self-esteem, I either took what was given to me or learned to live with what I had. When you ask for something, you have to believe it's yours to begin with. If you don't believe in it, who will?

One of the reasons we get rejected is because our approach is weak. If you lack confidence, it shows in your attitude. You can't fake it. You are more likely to make a good case if you believe it is yours.

4. Develop an attitude of gratitude for what you are getting

This isn't the same as "being satisfied with what you get." But the reality is that you may ask for ten dollars and get five. You ask for a week off and you get five days. You ask for a kiss and you get a handshake.

We have to appreciate the fact that what we want isn't always what people are willing to give. Patience is part of the game, and if you lose your patience or go from asking to demanding, you could end up losing everything.

5. Visualize your "big ask"

Visualization is a powerful technique that can prepare your mind for what it is about to do. It is so powerful that athletes, negotiators, and presidents visualize the success they want to achieve and the outcome before they take action.

Visualization is your mind's training for action in the near future. If you can visualize it, you can have it. Or at the very least, you can get your mind to take action.

World-renowned actor and comedian Jim Carrey improvised a powerful visualization technique when he was struggling as an actor in Hollywood.

In 1985, with dreams of becoming a famous actor in Hollywood, Carrey wrote himself a check for $10 million for "acting services rendered. He kept it in his wallet, postdated for ten years. Carrey went on to be paid millions for big blockbuster movies like Ace Ventura and Liar Liar.

6. Visualize the commitment as a positive experience

When I first tried this, I visualized the other person becoming confrontational and angry. This created intense feelings of stress and anger. So even when I got up the courage to ask, I did it in a very aggressive way. I wasn't asking, I was demanding. The other person felt this hostility and reacted in a similar state.

Under these circumstances, even if you get what you want, you'll damage your relationship with that person and kill any chance of future "win-win" situations. You may get what you want, but at a cost.

Visualize your "asking moment" as a positive, calm approach to the situation. It may not turn out the way you want, but going in with guns blazing is a sure way to kill any negotiation.

7. Know that you have nothing to lose

When you are preparing to ask or approach someone, always

tell yourself that you have nothing to lose: there is only gain, even if you get a NO.

Asking for things is like any other skill: it gets better over time. The more you do it, the better you get at it. You can only lose by not asking.

One of the obstacles that creates hesitation and prevents us from taking action is the distorted belief that if we are turned down, it will feel worse than death, as if we've lost something vitally important. But, as I have said, there is nothing to lose if you take courage and do something about it.

8. Know that rejection starts in your mind

Most of how we react is based on how we perceive ourselves and how we understand the situation. When you are rejected, you can make it all about you and tell yourself that it's because you are no good, worthless, and deserve to be rejected because you are unworthy.

The other way to look at it is to see it as a moment when the person isn't ready to accept your offer; they're not ready yet, no matter how much or how badly you beg.

People change from day to day. What they want one day isn't what they want the next. If you take rejection personally, you are setting yourself up for future suffering. The rejection you have labeled is all in your mind. You have to choose yourself in those moments and realize that there will be other opportunities and circumstances to ask someone else.

9. Project your confidence

You will have a much better chance of success if you ask with confidence. Ask as if you really mean it and have already gotten a YES. People who lack confidence act as if they don't really want what they are trying to get. The requestor picks up on this and is less likely to agree to your terms.

You can convey this confidence before you even say anything. Pay attention to your body language, eye contact, and voice control.

Do you sound confident? Do you look confident? Do you smell confident (people can "smell" fear)? Project the attitude of confidence with self-talk before you do anything. Pump yourself up and remind yourself that you have nothing to lose.

You get what you ask for

When I was in college, I interviewed for a part-time weekend job at a construction site. In the interview, the owner had asked me, "If we hire you, how much do you expect to be paid?" I didn't want to risk not getting hired by asking too much, even though I knew the work would be hard, so I quoted a price just above minimum wage.

I was hired and paid the price I asked, which at the time was just over $6 an hour. I felt pretty good about it because I had negotiated my wage and the manager had accepted it.

A few weeks later, I found out that one of the other workers who had been hired right after me was getting almost $2 more an hour! I approached the owner and asked why I was being treated so unfairly when we were both doing the same job. He simply said, "I asked you how much you wanted. We are paying you what you asked for. The other guy is also getting what he asked for."

That was a powerful lesson that stayed with me for years.

You always get what you ask for. When it comes to rejection, as you already know, most of us will do anything to avoid being rejected, even if it means devaluing ourselves.

Another lesson to learn is that not only do you get what you ask for in life, but you also get what you don't ask for... and that usually means nothing!

If you wait for others to figure out what you want, you'll go without the things you really want. Meanwhile, those who get ahead seize the moment and ask again and again and again for what they believe they deserve.

There is a saying: "Good things come to those who wait." I think this statement has a negative connotation - you could wait patiently for your day to come, for the right person to show up with the right opportunity, but it will come at a cost. You might end up getting what is left over from the people who got there before you. "The early bird gets the worm" is a better expression to live by.

Think about all the things you are not asking for in your life. Chances are you could fill a page right now. So, this is what we are going to do, right now. Take a piece of paper and make a list of all the things you want to ask for but have been afraid to. This can be anything from things at work to family issues.

Here are some prompts to get you started:

- "What am I afraid to ask my spouse for?"
- "What am I afraid to ask my coworkers?"
- "What am I afraid to ask a complete stranger?"
- "What am I afraid to ask my neighbor?"
- "What am I afraid to ask my teachers?"
- "What am I afraid to ask myself?"

Everyone has something they are afraid to ask for. Once you have clearly identified the things you are afraid to ask for, you can move on to the next phase:

"Why?"

Next to the list of things you are afraid to ask for, write down the reason you are afraid to ask. This is the fuel that will move you to action. Knowing what you are afraid to ask for is the first step because it makes you aware of what you are hiding from. But the why should make you at least a little angry.

"Don't waste energy trying to cover up failure. Learn from your failures and go on to the next challenge. It's okay to fail. If you're not failing, you're not growing."

—H. Stanley Judd

11

Asking for Help

*"Rejection is merely a redirection;
a course correction to your destiny.*

—Bryant McGill

When it comes to asking for help, there is a certain level of resistance that stands between you and the person you are reaching out to. When you ask another person for help, you are making yourself completely vulnerable. It feels like you are giving them permission to take full advantage of you. How terrifying!

What if they say NO? What if they tell you you're just not good enough to be helped? These sound like crazy responses to a reasonable request ("Hey, would you mind giving me a hand?"), but rejection plays crazy games with the mind.

When you ask for help, especially for men, there is this stigma that says asking for help is tantamount to admitting you can't do something. When you admit that you can't do something, it's the same as saying, "I can't handle it. You may equate asking for help with being weak or incompetent.

But that's not the case. Everyone needs help with something. And most people need help every day, but they don't ask for it. I remember once walking around the big city of Tokyo looking for a certain place. When it became obvious how lost I was,

I had no choice but to stop someone and ask for directions. Before I did that, I went through this thought:

- What if they don't stop?
- What if they laugh?
- What if they say, "Sorry, I can't help you."

It sounds exaggerated, but this is how the rejector thinks. We go through a list of possible scenarios that lead to the worst-case scenario in every situation. And it always comes back to the same thing: "What if I get rejected? It will crush me."

So, what did I do?

I asked someone

The first person didn't quit. The next person I asked did. Not only did they tell me where the place was, they went out of their way to personally show me right up to the front door.

Where would I have ended up if I hadn't asked? Lost and confused and kicking myself for not asking.

Asking for help, as scary as it may seem, is perfectly natural. In fact, when I think about it, I was always happy to lend a hand myself in any situation where someone needed help. It was a chance to be of service to another human being. By giving, you always receive, and if you don't receive, you're still ahead of the game.

You see, I was always afraid to ask anyone for anything. If I needed help with something, I would find a way so I wouldn't have to ask. If someone saw me struggling, I would tell him or her, "It's okay, I got it. But the truth is, I wanted their help; I just couldn't admit it. I was always afraid that if I accepted someone's help, I would owe them, and I would never be able to pay them back. I didn't want to seem needy or incompetent.

So, go ahead and ask someone for help. Better yet, offer to help someone if it looks like they need it. Not everyone will ask for it, and they may even reject it when you try to give it to them.

Here are a few things to start with:

- Ask someone to help you fix your car.
- Ask someone to help you lift something.
- Ask someone to help you with your homework.
- Ask someone to help you solve a difficult problem.
- Ask someone to show you the way to your hotel because you're lost.
- Ask someone to lend you some money because you forgot your wallet today.
- Ask someone to help you carry something heavy.

Now, what kind of help are you going to ask someone for?

Now it is up to you.

Write down twenty ideas of things you can ask for this week. You can also reflect on last week and come up with ideas of things you could have asked for but didn't. Chances are they will come up again.

Another exercise you can try is a self-analysis exercise. Look at areas of your life that you are afraid to approach. This could be a relationship or a situation at work. Maybe you can't handle asking people for help no matter what. You are afraid of looking stupid. Take note of the areas from which you withdraw.

Then ...

Pick one of your fears and focus on it. Think about how you are going to ask for that one thing. Feel the fear working its way through you. How are you going to ask for it? Who are you going to ask? When will you ask?

So here is my **simple 6-step process for asking for what you want:**

1. Write down in a notebook or Evernote the one thing you really want.
2. Make a short list of three people who could give it to you.
3. Write down the benefit of asking them for what you want.
4. Ask confidently, as if you already have it.
5. Be respectful of their decision if it doesn't turn out the way you wanted.
6. Finally, let go of your expectations.

You can make a huge difference in your life by asking the right people for the right things at the right time. Make a commitment to ask for at least one thing you want once a day. It can be something you want for yourself, or better yet, help someone else get something they want.

Nothing happens in life unless you ask for it. If you want it, you have to go out there and tell people. We can do this by asking for what is important.

Now think very carefully about the one thing that you want right now, but you're afraid to ask for. How are you going to ask? To whom are you going to ask? When are you going to ask? There has to be a plan to make it happen. You have to decide what, where, and who. Once you know that half, the work is done.

Create a benefit chart: Why it pays to ask

Create a benefit chart. On one side, list the benefits of not asking. On the other side, list the benefits of asking. This is your win-win chart. Measure both sides and see how rejection is holding you back.

Asking For Help

What you can do is write down exactly what you are going to ask for and then how you are going to do it. How are you going to ask? What are you going to say? When will you ask for it? Question yourself and get pumped up and excited about asking for the things you deserve and want.

PART 3

THE POWER OF DESENSITIZATION

12

Desensitization and the Flooding Process

"When you're not putting yourself out there, you're rejecting yourself by default."

—Jia Jiang, bestselling author of
Rejection Proof

You think you are protecting yourself when you avoid situations that are potentially harmful to your ego, confidence, and pride.

In fact, what appears to be a protective cocoon actually becomes a personal prison created not to protect you, but to isolate your fear from experiencing what it needs to get out of the way.

In this final section of the book, we will take a look at how desensitization works and how to put it into practice so that you can numb your fear of rejection.

In psychology, desensitization is defined as "the diminished emotional responsiveness to a negative or aversive stimulus after repeated exposure to it." It also occurs when an emotional response is repeatedly evoked in situations where the action tendency associated with the emotion proves irrelevant or unnecessary.

Jia Jiang and 100 Days of Rejection

Could you imagine putting yourself into a state of Rejection Proof, where you commit to provoking rejection for 100 days in order to numb yourself to its negative effects?

This is what Jia Jiang did in his Rejection Journey. Dubbed the "Rejection Whisperer," Jiang set out to intentionally get rejected for 100 days in order to overcome rejection by throwing himself at it over and over again.

From a young age, Jia Jiang fantasized about being an entrepreneur. After receiving a rejection email from a potential investor for one of his inventions that would launch his entrepreneurial business, Jiang set out to "thrive in the face of fear," as he said. And the experiment was on.

Over the next 100 days, recording each attempt on his phone, Jiang tried some pretty crazy experiments in his attempt to get rejected.

Some of the best ways he tried to get rejected were:

- Asking a security guard for $100
- Asking to make an announcement over the PA system at Costco
- Asking a barber if he could cut her hair
- Asking a donut shop for a special donut shaped like the Olympic rings
- Be a tour guide at a museum
- Sell cookies for the Girl Scouts
- Find a job in one day
- Be a greeter at Starbucks
- Get a haircut at PetSmart
- Challenge a CEO to a staring contest

You can check out Jia's website at **rejectiontherapy.com** and the videos documenting his **100 days of rejection**.

But what's so important about Jia Jiang's social experiment on rejection isn't that he did something that's rarely been done before, but that he changed and evolved as a result. He learned with each lesson and attempt at rejection.

The lesson Jiang shares is crucial to understanding why people reject you. You see, when you're in a situation where you're rejected, told no, or basically given the bad news that you're just not good enough for the "team," it feels like a personal attack on your character. Think about the last time you had a really bad rejection. If you are like me, it was like getting stabbed repeatedly, but on an emotional scale.

In his book *Rejection Proof*, Jiang explains:

> *"I had always thought of my rejection as a kind of rare disease, like guinea worm, which causes terrible pain but affects only a tiny fraction of the population."*

I can relate, and I am sure you can, too. But isn't it true that when you experience some form of rejection, whether it's personal or business, it somehow feels like it's all about you? That somehow there is something special about you that caused it and that no one else is going through anything remotely similar?

Let's look at it another way. If you are auditioning for a musical and there are 500 performers, only one person is going to be chosen. It may or may not be you, but regardless, 499 people will be rejected.

The same goes for interviews, dating, and submitting a book to a publisher. Someone is going to be rejected. It's a relief to know it's not just you.

Jia Jiang also says:

"Outside influences have a huge impact on the way people see a situation - and those influences can change over time. The way someone feels about me or a request I'm making can be influenced by factors that have nothing to do with me. If people's behavior and opinions can change so drastically based on so many factors, why should I take everything about a rejection so personally?"

We are sensitive people by nature. And rejection is the virus that has raised that sensitivity to a boiling point. The fear we have that is labeled "fear of rejection" is really a deep and personal fear of ourselves.

How "I" feels after being rejected is ten times worse than what other people think. But when it happens, shame kicks in. This, attached to a highly sensitive individual, makes everything that happens personal.

But as Jiang says, *"There are so many variables and reasons for not being accepted that are far beyond our control."*

Beautiful, highly intelligent, rich and powerful people struggle with the same thing. People we look at and think "she has nothing to worry about" because of her appearance or social status.

But it comes back to this: I have yet to meet a perfect individual who was able to get everything they wanted or be liked by everyone. The next time you think that, check to see if they have wings on their back, because everyone is vulnerable.

Everyone has flaws. But we learn how to deal with them. And by focusing on personal development as a way to keep moving forward, you can combat your feelings of inadequacy. When you are rejected for something, you can ask for feedback as to why you received a NO.

By getting feedback and better understanding the reason for the decision, you can use that information to focus on strengthening a weakness. I wouldn't get plastic surgery if someone didn't like the way I looked, but if it's a skill I can improve on, like public speaking, there are always ways to make it better.

You may be feeding yourself these lies:

- "I was rejected because I'm ugly."
- "I was rejected because I'm not smart enough."
- "I was rejected because I can't be loved."

The list of lies goes on and on. But none of them are true.

So how do we get to the point in our lives where we can move beyond this illusion and begin to feel better about who we are?

You already know the answer. From the beginning of this book, we have talked about how to choose yourself above any situation, how to face difficult moments when failure is imminent, and how to ask for what you want in order to break through that barrier.

But here is the thing. People's fear is not the problem. For years I thought people were the problem, and if I could just figure them out, I'd be less afraid of criticism and judgment. But it wasn't.

Rejection rarely has anything to do with someone else and has more to do with how we feel about ourselves. As Jiang said, the judgments and decisions people make are based on their feelings, attitudes, needs, and wants in the moment. If you don't have what they are looking for, they will find someone who does.

Understanding this one concept cuts our fear in half. When you look at it this way, you could say that rejection doesn't really exist. It is a self-created condition that is rarely controlled by anyone but yourself.

"When you give yourself permission to communicate what matters to you in every situation you will have peace despite rejection or disapproval. Putting a voice to your soul helps you to let go of the negative energy of fear and regret."

—Shannon L. Alder

13

Getting Desensitized to Rejection

"There are two wrong reactions to a rejection slip: deciding it's a final judgment on your story and/or talent and deciding it's no judgment on your story and/or talent."

—Nancy Kress

When I finished high school, I had a job in construction, and most of the work we did was outdoors. In the winter, the temperature would drop to about minus fifteen or twenty.

Those are cold conditions to work outside six hours a day. But after a few days you got used to it. The first couple of days the feeling of the cold was intense, but over the course of a couple of days you never thought about it.

You get used to the conditions you're exposed to over a period of time, and your body will condition itself to adverse situations after a certain amount of exposure.

Even now, almost twenty years later, the cold doesn't bother me as much as it does most people I know. My exposure to harsh temperatures hardened my attitude toward adverse conditions.

The same principle works for most things we fear, including rejection. We fear what we understand least, and if you are struggling with your personal rejection issues, it is because you have avoided putting yourself in the path of direct fire. In other words, what we run from doesn't go away; it just buries itself deeper. What you resist persists.

Facing and defeating rejection works in a similar way. You can reduce its power by conditioning yourself through exposure to rejection. This is what it means to desensitize yourself.

Desensitizing yourself to the fear of rejection means taking intentional action against the events or situations that you fear the most.

Desensitization is practiced by conditioning your mind with repeated attempts to be rejected. Based on respondent conditioning, it is a form of behavioral therapy used by psychiatrists to help people overcome deep fears and phobias. Also known as flooding, this type of practice can be used to condition yourself for rejection.

As we discussed earlier, Jia Jiang gives an amazing account of how he set himself up to be intentionally rejected over the course of a hundred days. His goal was to get so used to being rejected that he no longer felt anything about it.

There is a lesson to be learned here that says What we do repeatedly becomes second nature.

This could also be called mastering rejection. You get so used to it that soon it is no longer an issue.

Another interesting experiment I tried is called Rejection Therapy, a systematic approach to mastering rejection originally created by entrepreneur Jason Comely. The rules of the game are as follows:

You have to be rejected by someone at least once a day. More specifically, you have to be rejected, not just try to be rejected, but do something that will get you rejected.

If you go out there and try, but your attempt at rejection fails, it doesn't count. Getting rejected is SUCCESS in this

Rejection Therapy game. If your rejection is accepted, you can assume that you didn't ask for enough.

Can you imagine how you would feel after thirty days if you deliberately put yourself in a position that challenged your comfort zone and pushed your fear of being told NO to the limit?

That is what desensitization is all about. You have bought into rejection because, like many people, you have spent your life trying to avoid it. Hiding from it and protecting yourself makes you weaker, not stronger.

Don't you think it's time to do something about it? I know I do.

What you can do right now is make a list of all the crazy ways you can be rejected. This can be a simple request; start small if you want. Build up to it. Take small steps every day to desensitize yourself. Each day try to push the envelope a little further. See how many ideas you can come up with.

Then, at the beginning of each morning, choose the one you will implement today. Again, you can make up your own rules. You can do it the Rejection Therapy way and only count it as a success IF you get rejected, or you can give yourself credit for trying regardless of the outcome.

Create Your Own Rejection Challenge

What ideas can you come up with to desensitize and reduce your fear of rejection?

Here are a few things I have tried:

- I went to a computer store and asked if I could borrow a computer for the weekend because mine was broken. Result: They said no, but that I could buy a used computer for a very low price (at their store, of course).

- I asked someone I didn't know if I could stay at their house for a week because mine was being renovated. Result: They said NO, but offered to help me find a cheap hotel.
- I asked the police if I could ride with them in their patrol car. Result: They said NO, but that if I went to the station and made a request, it would probably be granted. I didn't do that because I knew it was a no-brainer, but I did ask for something I would never have tried before the game.
- I went to an all-female yoga studio and asked to join. Result: They said NO (of course), but directed me to a co-ed yoga studio.

Challenge Your Rejection

Now why don't you challenge yourself to try. See how many situations you can think of where you put yourself in a situation where you might be rejected.

Here are **10 fun challenges** to get you started:

1. **Approach ten people** at random and complement each of them. This could be something they are wearing, their hairstyle, or a personal characteristic you have noticed.
2. **Go to a furniture store** and ask if you can take a twenty-minute power nap on one of their model beds.
3. **Meet with your employer** or boss at work and ask if you can start leaving work thirty minutes earlier to spend more time at home with your family.
4. **Tell someone it's your birthday** and ask them to sing Happy Birthday to you.

5. In a supermarket or coffee shop, **ask if you can "go to the front of the line"** because you have "no patience."
6. Next time you check in for a flight, **ask to be upgraded** to first class without paying extra.
7. Challenge someone to a **staring contest**. You must hold the stare for at least one minute.
8. Ask your manager or the CEO of the company if you can **work in their office for a day** because you think it will help you be more productive.
9. **Draw a picture**. It can be anything. You can add color or be as creative as you want. Then carry it around with you for the day and whenever you meet someone, show them the drawing and ask, "So, what do you think?"
10. Ask a **random couple on the street to tell you** the story of how they met.

"Rejection doesn't have to mean you aren't good enough; it often just means the other person failed to notice what you have to offer."

—Ash Sweeney

14

No More Excuses

"Just get out there and get rejected, and sometimes it's going to get dirty. But that's OK, 'cause you're going to feel great after, you're going to feel like, 'Wow. I disobeyed fear.'"

—Jason Comely

You have to take a little risk of the ego or you'll stay where you are. If you don't, you have no one to blame but yourself. Small steps make real progress over time.

Taking no steps keeps you stuck. Even if you make small progress every day, that's still better than the other 99% of people out there doing nothing.

Most people talk about the things they want to do and end up making excuses for why they can't do them. Excuses are another way we keep ourselves trapped. You can free yourself by throwing out the outdated reasoning that feeds the lie of what you can or cannot do.

- "I'll do it when I have enough time…"
- "I'll do it when I save more money…"
- "I'll do it when I finish school…"
- "I'll do it when the kids are gone…"

But those "some days" never come, and in the end they live meager lives and give up their dreams, throwing everything away for the hope of something that never comes.

Their excuses reinforce the possibility of rejection. We make excuses because we fear negative consequences.

- "What if it doesn't work out?"
- "What if they don't approve my application?"
- "What if I don't finish what I started?"
- "What if I get stuck?"
- "What if I fail?"

I have always strived to make a better life for myself, but I have gotten stuck many times along the way. I stayed stuck for many years, stuck in jobs, wasting time in dead-end relationships, stuck in various addictions, and living my life like someone who didn't care much about themselves.

I wasn't just killing time, I was killing myself and my life

The bottom line: You owe it to yourself to live BIG. There is no satisfaction in living small and hiding from the world. You can put yourself out there by choosing who you want to be and accepting who you are right now.

There are no more lies or illusions when you choose to take charge of your life.

When you choose NOT to believe the lies, you take a positive action toward inner healing. You stop playing the victim and take charge. You can only do this when you make a conscious decision to evolve beyond your current state, which may be giving in to your weaker state that keeps you stuck and trapped.

Put yourself out there. Take a risk and talk to strangers. Do things you have never tried before. What do you have to lose? You see, one of the things that holds us back is believing that there is something to lose by taking a risk.

You are on a mission to engage in the full human experience by putting everything on the line. Try the things you are afraid to do. You won't lose anything, I swear. You will only gain, even if you fail or are rejected.

Don't focus on the outcome. Lower your expectations. Expecting everything to work out will scare you into doing nothing. You'll suffer from action paralysis.

Here are some examples:

- You start a YouTube channel to document your blogs or tell people how your week is going, make it a mini-documentary.
- You call people you would normally avoid.
- You talk openly with people about whatever is on your mind.
- You introduce yourself to random people at the grocery store.
- Tell your spouse and children that you love them.
- Admit that you are not perfect and that you make mistakes.
- You try to do the one thing you swore you'd never do.
- You make it a daily habit to ask for at least one thing you want.

Your conditioned response can be mastered by desensitizing and conditioning your mind to handle the bad things when they happen. You can, over time, condition your mind to adapt to being told NO, "Go away," "You're no good," whatever people throw at you, you'll be ready to take it.

But it will be hard at first. Our fear of being rejected, like any fear, is all-powerful until we take all the power it has over us.

You must prove to yourself that fear is a lie. You can instill in yourself the confidence that there's nothing wrong with the world and that you'll get through this no matter what.

Here is an example. You have an idea for a business that you want to start. But you only think about it and never act on it. You're afraid of failing. What would it take for you to start the one thing you have always been afraid to do? What would be the first step you could take? What would be the smallest first step you could take?

We get overwhelmed when we think of all the big things. So how about breaking it down as small as you can? Not everything has to be done in one big leap.

Think about where you'd be in six months and work toward a plan that produces real results. How would you feel in a few weeks if you suddenly took charge, put yourself out there, and started taking action on the fears that are holding you back?

I can tell you from personal experience: Rejection would lose all power over you. In fact, you'd wonder what you were afraid of in the first place. But you have to start somewhere.

When you realize that rejection has less to do with you as a person and more to do with the demands and dynamics of the situation and how people are feeling at the moment, it becomes so much easier to just put yourself out there, it becomes easier to deal with it.

That's just the way things are; we don't live in a perfect world. In a perfect world everybody gets along and gets what they want. In the real world, we know that's not the case. When we understand this bitter pill of reality, we can see our life problems and fears as less personal.

Toughen up and face the rejection that made you afraid. Most of the time, rejection is nothing more than an emotional response to a situation that you disapprove of or that disapproves of you.

Action Plan: The 60-Day Rejected on Purpose Challenge

Here is what you will do. As you follow this system, over the next few days and weeks, you will see that rejection only lives within you. It exists nowhere else. No one can reject you better than you can reject yourself.

- Make a list of all the things you avoid because of your fear of rejection.
- Now that you have your list, you're going to start doing those things.
- What would you do first if you knew you couldn't be rejected?

A mentor of mine suggested this and it was a miraculous step. I had never done it before, but after I completed that simple action step, it was easy to look around and see what I could actually do to overcome my rejected self. It was like a road map I had created, a checklist of sorts, where I could go down the list and start checking things off as I did them.

Here is what you do

Taking action against the things that scare you empowers your senses like nothing else. It pulls you out of the safety zone you have built to protect yourself. Your comfort zone is a survival cushion. Sometimes we need the protection it provides, but most of the time we stay there and never move forward.

Imagine how many opportunities you will create starting today by doing the things that have always scared you.

- Will you write a book?
- Will you create a video and post on Social Media?

- Start interacting with people more instead of shying away from them (I'm not talking about social media, but real interaction).
- Do a job interview you've been avoiding?
- Test drive a sports car even though you don't have the money to buy it?
- Talk to someone you've been avoiding?

Take action and do it every day. If you're afraid and think you'll fail, do it anyway. Taking charge of your life is an action, not an event. You seize the day when you seize the moment. No one gives you a map to follow; the only map is the one you create today.

- Will you live as a free individual?
- Are you ready to be free of rejection?

Action Plan

Take thirty minutes to think of all the ways you can push yourself to take action on something you wouldn't normally do. If your fear of rejection is in relationships, you may have rejection issues with men or women. If your rejection issues are centered around acceptance, you may have difficulty joining groups or events that focus on community or social activities.

But there is another way to play this game. In your daily life, take note of all the opportunities you have to try something, and you don't. You want to, but you hesitate because you're afraid or you think you'll fail.

Jot these situations down in your memory and then try to take a chance on them. You may find, as I did, that your rejection-centered self is controlled by fear in several situations. Once you identify what these situations are, you can develop a strategy to take action in that area.

For example, I had a great fear of public speaking. I avoided it at all costs. So I put myself in a situation where I had to give a speech and openly discuss something in public.

My other fear was meeting new people. With vulnerability issues, I made myself vulnerable. At first, I had a physical reaction to this approach with sweating and shaking. But after trying it ten times, I went from fear to desensitization to rejection.

Try it and you will see that it works. You can get the freedom to be yourself, and then as you take more risks by putting yourself out there, you'll experience a new freedom you never had before. I remember feeling that the loneliness I carried with me every day was mostly of my own making. Focusing on desensitization strategies healed me from the pain of isolation.

For me, this was the freedom I had always sought.

You can have that, too.

Conclusion: Building the Rejection Free Lifestyle

*"I think that you have to believe in your destiny;
that you will succeed, you will meet a lot of rejection
and it is not always a straight path, there will
be detours—so enjoy the view."*

—Michael York

You can create your own lifestyle, experience a transformation, or make choices that take you in a completely new direction. You are as free as you choose to be. By challenging fear and doing what scares you, rejection no longer has power over you. You can gain power through the power of thought, confidence, and pushing your self-esteem to new levels.

Before we part ways, I want to leave you with three final lessons from this book. But before I do, let me say that this is a fascinating journey we are on. What makes it so interesting is that we are given so many opportunities to live life the way we want to.

THREE FINAL LESSONS

Lesson #1: Tell Your Story

For many years I didn't think I had anything interesting to say. I was always afraid I'd be boring, or that people would dismiss my opinions or ideas as stupid or unintellectual.

Then I became a good storyteller. I practiced telling stories in a way that engaged people. I did this not to be more popular or to get all the attention; I did it because I genuinely like people and want to share my own life lessons.

One of the biggest reasons I write about rejection and share this experience with you is so that we can learn from each other's journeys. Everyone has a story to tell and it is important that you get your story out there. You never know what impact you might have on a life.

Listen to the message people are trying to get across. If you show a genuine interest in someone, they'll really open up and share their dreams and aspirations. This is the beginning of a good relationship.

Many relationships start out shallow and lacking in depth. People are afraid to get close or to let their guard down. You can have the advantage by showing genuine interest and getting to know the other person through sharing experiences.

Lesson #2: Put your flaws in perspective

This is a self-improvement book. I hope you have found it useful and can apply it to your life right now. Just keep in mind that self-improvement doesn't mean self-perfection.

We rejectionists really beat ourselves up. We spend years asking ourselves, "What's wrong with me? Why am I so different?" You are not so different. It's just that everyone else is trying so hard to be normal that it feels that way.

We all have flaws. That's okay. You've been living with those flaws up until now, and that's okay, too. With this book, I hope you can overcome and manage some of your flaws; other flaws we cannot change, or they may take more time to heal.

There is no rush. You have time. One day at a time and you'll make it. You can accept yourself as you are, flaws and golden points. You may feel embarrassed or ashamed. But what are your good points? What makes you unique and precious? List them and remind yourself what they are.

Lesson #3: Take Consistent Action

Nothing will happen to change your fears, and therefore your life, unless you make the changes. To do this, you must focus on the changes you want to see in your life as a result of your choices.

Do you want to stay trapped or break free? Will you explore the unknowns of your true self or stay hidden behind a veil of fear that keeps you doing the same thing over and over again? Will you take action or wait for action to be taken against you?

The key to creating lasting change is doing something repeatedly over a long period of time. It is the same with creating habits. Do something for a few weeks and you'll gain some momentum, but if you stop, the habit you're trying to replace will return. You can start changing your life today by taking a small action every day. Ask for something you want; take a small risk; read a book on personal development.

Stay focused on your path to becoming Rejection Free and you'll soon find yourself living a new life in a different way.

I know you'll do what's best. Do it for yourself. Do what you've always wanted to do but lacked the courage to do. Know that you can do anything you want if you have the courage to take action.

Evaluate where you are in your life and take the first step forward. Just one step is enough. For today.

Small steps add up to big gains over time.

Ask for what you want.
Help people get what they want.
Be who you are, not who the world thinks you should be.
You have this, now.
You have a choice. Now go out there, seize the moment and live your life the way it was meant to be.
Life is too short to be afraid.
Defeat rejection and live the Rejection Free lifestyle.
I'll see you there...
Scott Allan

"There is no failure except no longer trying There is no defeat except from within, no really insurmountable barrier save our own inherent weakness of purpose."

—Ken Hubbard